THE MARVELS OF FLYING

Air Travel before 1950

Andrew Emmerson

In the mid-1930s flights left Croydon Airport for South Africa every Tuesday and Friday. Passengers in this picture are boarding the Handley Page HP42 airliner of Imperial Airways after arriving from the central London air terminal on the AEC Regal bus seen in the background.

Cover image: The De Havilland aerodrome at Hatfield (Herts) in 1936. Established primarily for evaluating aircraft constructed at De Havilland's factory, it was also used for a flying school and the headquarters of the London Flying Club.

ACKNOWLEDGEMENTS

Grateful thanks go to all those who provided assistance, in particular the British Postal Museum, Dudley Brown, David Cockle, Graham Feakins, David Hayward, Andrew Henderson, Mike Horne, Neil Johannessen, David Marden, Sandy Skinner, Julian Stray and the World War II Railway Study Group.

Photo credits are as follows: Alamy (page 18 lower), The Automobile Association (page 73), Bluebell Railway Museum (page 55), Dell & Wainwright/RIBA Library Photographs Collection (page 31), Getty Images (pages 14, 24, 25, 51 upper, 54, 71, 83), Mary Evans Picture Library (pages 16 lower, 27, 30, 57, 69 right), Science & Society Picture Library (page 19), Stilltime Collection (page 37), TfL from the London Transport Museum collection (page 69 left), Upacut Archive (pages 7, 60, 62) and Wikimedia Commons (page 6 upper, 11, 21, 63, 74, 82). The remainder of the illustrations are from public domain sources or the author's own collection. A number of the photographs are taken from period documents and may not match today's reproduction standards.

First published 2013
ISBN 978-1-85414-371-6
Published by Capital Transport Publishing Ltd
www.capitaltransport.com
Printed by Parksons Graphics
© Capital Transport Publishing Ltd 2013

CONTENTS

This is the 'London Air Port' in 1926, then located at Croydon. In those days passengers walked to the aircraft across the apron while their luggage followed by hand cart. Only two years later the rather primitive wood structures had been swept away and replaced by the substantial terminal building that still stands today as Airport House.

THE DAWN OF AIR TRAVEL

The year 1919 marked the beginning of civilian air travel in Britain. A company with the title Aircraft Transport & Travel Limited, exploiting military aviation experience gained during World War One, became the first airline to operate regular international passenger flights, between London and Paris. Without government support, the company began its regular service from Hounslow Heath aerodrome (south west of London) and Paris (Le Bourget) on 25 August 1919. Its reputation for reliability secured it the first British civil air mail contract from the Post Office in November of that year. Another route followed the next year, from London (Croydon) to Amsterdam in 1920 on behalf of Dutch state airline KLM. Debt problems soon forced this pioneer company into liquidation but its services survived, being continued by Daimler Airway Ltd.

State support

Even though the beginnings of air travel were marked by primitive aircraft and airports, the growth of this fledgling industry could not be halted. New airlines, both British and foreign, entered the arena. Competition was keen and to some eyes unfair, since the most aggressive countries (France and Germany) operated state airlines or offered their carriers state subsidies. British interests were being undermined, especially as state support for aviation could facilitate overseas trade and settlement by improving travel to and from the colonies. With this in mind the British government arranged the merger of four independent airlines in 1923 to create a national airline of sufficient substance to develop Britain's external air services unhindered by foreign operators. Encouraged by a subsidy of £1 million over ten years, Imperial Airways Limited was formed on 31 March 1924. Its operations were based at Croydon (then known as the London Airport), focused on serving overseas destinations, leaving internal British services to other operators.

Overseas expansion

Within five years Imperial Airways offered services to Paris, Brussels, Basle, Cologne and Zurich. However, its main focus was on developing routes to the Empire — to South Africa, India and ultimately Australia. Development took two directions: the Africa and Eastern routes. The Eastern was the first to be developed and employed a combination of rail journeys and flights. The first service to India (Karachi) was opened in March 1929, with the journey taking seven days; it was extended to Delhi in December of the same year. Significant service improvement and expansion of these Empire routes took place in the 1930s, as we shall see in the next chapter.

Britain's pioneer airline, Aircraft Transport & Travel Ltd, operated aircraft like this De Havilland-designed Airco DH16, seen around 1920 probably at Croydon Airport.

Opposite: Up close and personal. In 1926 there was not a huge amount of room to move in British airliners. The woven rattan seats in this Handley Page W10 aircraft were probably a lot more comfortable than perhaps they might appear.

The decidedly rural aspect of Croydon Airport in 1926. Note the control tower, looking for all the world like a railway signal cabin.

Aircraft were small and slow at this time. Typical of mid-1920s passenger craft was the Handley Page W10, a medium-range biplane airliner used by Imperial Airways. Equipped with seats for 16 passengers and an on-board lavatory, it was used on Imperial's Silver Wings service from London (Croydon Airport) to Paris, Brussels, Cologne and Zurich. Its cruising speed was 100mph, with a range of 500 miles. The 450hp of the two Napier Lion engines meant that a fully laden W10 needed to climb to 5,000 feet before crossing the English Channel, to ensure making a safe crossing in event of an engine failure.

This evocative cover art from a 1937 publication sums up the exotic appeal and excitement of air travel, with an autogiro high in the sky to add a touch of topicality.

The general aspect is somewhat reminiscent of Shoreham (Brighton-Worthing) Airport but the image is more stylised than specific.

AIR TRAVEL TAKES OFF

The 1930s saw considerable growth in the number of routes and airports, although not on today's scale. Many of the flights were both infrequent and of marginal utility (Romford to Clacton for instance), operated on a shoestring by independent operators. Some airlines closed their operations during the winter months, reflecting uncongenial weather and poor bookings. A substantial number of the airports were municipally owned and it could be said that some were more expressions of local pride than vital transport facilities.

Assured future

That air travel had a future was not in doubt, however, as newcomers to the skies demonstrated. Edward Hillman was a successful businessman, who by expansion and takeovers had built up an empire of bus and coach operations in east London and Essex. He also had aspirations of providing low-cost, 'no frills' air travel and when the newly formed London Transport forcibly acquired most of his bus fleet in 1933, he took the opportunity to use the compensation he received to expand Hillman's Airways with an international route from Romford (Maylands) to Paris. True to his philosophy, the fares charged were well below those fares charged by his rivals Air France and Imperial Airways. On 31 December 1934, however, he died and his airline was merged into the new British Airways conglomerate.

A new and much larger entrant to the air travel business was Railway Air Services Ltd, formed in 1934 by the four main railway companies of Britain and Imperial Airways with the remit 'to provide and operate air services in the British Isles and elsewhere, and to form connecting links with the services of Imperial Airways.' This was a shrewd move by the railways to take a share in all modes of public transport (they had already made substantial investments in the larger bus operators in 1929 and bought the road haulage carriers Pickfords and Carter Paterson in 1934).

RAS operated a number of cross-country routes along with what was its main trunk service between London (Croydon) and Glasgow, also serving Birmingham, Manchester or Liverpool and Belfast. In 1934 this service operated once daily in each direction and was particularly useful for passengers connecting at Croydon with Imperial flights to the Continent. Improvements made in 1939 included a direct through service between London, Manchester, Liverpool and Glasgow. Four air services were provided daily between Liverpool, Manchester and London, one of these being especially popular as it made a Continental connection at Croydon, enabling travellers to be in Paris before lunch.

Another newcomer was Aer Lingus, founded by the Irish government in 1936 to provide air services between Ireland and the United Kingdom. The airline's maiden flight was made on 27 May 1936 from Baldonnel Aerodrome in Dublin to Bristol (Whitchurch) airfield when a six-seater De Havilland Dragon

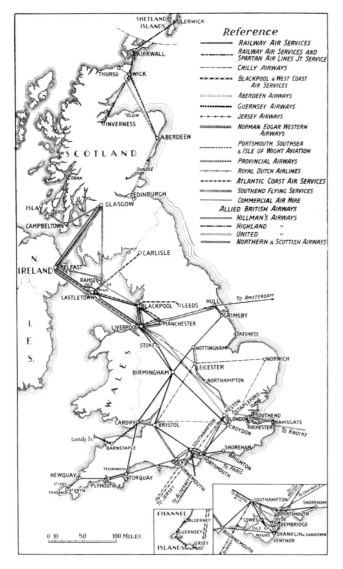

Reference

————	RAILWAY AIR SERVICES
—·—·—	RAILWAY AIR SERVICES AND SPARTAN AIR LINES JT. SERVICE
— — —	CRILLY AIRWAYS
—×—×—	BLACKPOOL & WEST COAST AIR SERVICES
:::::::::	ABERDEEN AIRWAYS
••••••••	GUERNSEY AIRWAYS
—+—+—	JERSEY AIRWAYS
∷∷∷∷∷	NORMAN EDGAR WESTERN AIRWAYS
··········	PORTSMOUTH, SOUTHSEA & ISLE OF WIGHT AVIATION
∴∴∴∴∴	PROVINCIAL AIRWAYS
—○—○—	ROYAL DUTCH AIRLINES
—+—+—	ATLANTIC COAST AIR SERVICES
▬▬▬▬	SOUTHEND FLYING SERVICES
————	COMMERCIAL AIR HIRE
	ALLIED BRITISH AIRWAYS
·—·—·	HILLMAN'S AIRWAYS
—·—·—	HIGHLAND ”
━━━	UNITED ”
∞∞∞∞	NORTHERN & SCOTTISH AIRWAYS

named *Iolar* (Eagle) carried just five passengers across the Irish Sea. Routes to Liverpool and the Isle of Man followed but the outbreak of war in 1939 hindered further expansion.

Many of the independent operators named on this map had amalgamated by 1939, however. In fact the swift expansion of air travel in Britain during the 1930s was matched by rapid consolidation of the airline operators, both by way of mergers and in commercial alliances. Passengers had to contend with many name changes during this period.

- In 1924, British Marine Air Navigation Co Ltd merged with Handley Page Transport, Instone Air Line and Daimler Airway to form Imperial Airways.
- In 1935, Spartan Air Lines and United Airways were merged to form Allied British Airways Ltd. This company merged with Hillman's Airways to form British Airways Ltd later that year.
- In 1936 British Continental Airways was added, with the British Airways name retained.
- In 1937 Scottish Airways Ltd was formed to merge the operations of Northern & Scottish Airlines with Highland Airways Ltd; British Airways Ltd held a 50 per cent stake.

By 1935, when this map was published, the pre-war airline routes were largely complete apart from the later service from Liverpool to Dublin, in the Irish Free State.

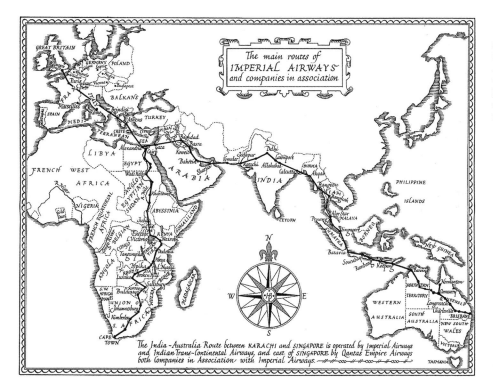

By 1935 an alliance of Imperial Airways and other airlines served much of the British Empire outside the Americas. The Atlantic Ocean remained a barrier to be overcome before Canada and the Caribbean could be reached, however.

International expansion

On Imperial Airways' Eastern Route passenger flights to India (Calcutta) began in 1933, the same year as its services reached Rangoon (Burma) and Singapore. Australia (Brisbane) was reached by passenger-carrying aircraft in 1935, the Australian airline QANTAS providing the link from Singapore to Brisbane. Hong Kong followed in 1936. New destinations served on the Africa Route began with Mwanza on Lake Victoria (Tanganyika) in 1931, whilst the first passenger service to Cape Town was offered in 1932. In February 1936 the trans-Africa route was opened between Khartoum and Kano (Nigeria), extended to Lagos in October of that year. The introduction of 'Empire' class flying boats in 1937 enabled the airline to offer a through (rather than piecemeal in stages) service to the Cape and the following year the same flying boats also flew between Britain and Australia via India and the Middle East.

Choice of operators

If the previous section gave the impression that Imperial Airways was the only airline flying beyond British waters, this must be corrected. At various times during the 1930s passengers flying to the Irish Republic had a choice between Aer Lingus (Liverpool or Croydon to Dublin) and Irish Sea Airways (Croydon or Cardiff to Dublin). To France you could fly with Air France (Croydon to Paris) or Olley Air Services Ltd (Croydon to Deauville), whilst to Belgium you could use Hillman's Airways (from Stapleford [Essex] to Ostend and Brussels (later British Airways from Croydon), or the Belgian national carrier SABENA between Croydon and Brussels. To The Netherlands KLM had operated a Croydon to Amsterdam service from 17 May 1920 onwards, a route also served by British Airways Ltd. KLM also operated routes to Amsterdam from Liverpool and Hull. The German Lufthansa operated a London–Amsterdam–Berlin service, whilst British Airways Ltd flew from Croydon to Hamburg. The same airline flew from Croydon to Copenhagen, a route shared with Danish Airlines (DDL), and to Malmö and Stockholm, a route shared with AB Aerotransport (ABA), which marked some of its craft Swedish Air Lines in 1939. Swiss Air Lines first flew from Zurich to London in 1936 (a route offered by Imperial Airways since 1929), whilst Avio Linee Italiane extended its Venice–Milan–Turin –Paris route to London in 1938.

Rate of growth of traffic

The growing number of passengers inevitably put pressure on the airports, the smaller of which were really quite basic and cramped. Already in 1934 the prominent Scottish author, journalist and later Science Editor of the *News Chronicle* newspaper Ritchie Calder wrote:

> 'Before aviation can become really popular and practical, the need for huge aerodromes for landing and taking off must be met. Those can be provided only outside the big towns or in the open country, with the result that two hours out of the four it takes to get from London to Paris are wasted in travelling to Croydon and from Le Bourget. The same applies everywhere.'

By the late 1930s the pressure was being felt, with London's Croydon and Heston airports barely able to cope. Ambitious (but unfulfilled) plans were conceived to build additional airports on London's periphery, as described in the chapter *Flights of Fancy*, with resolution coming only after the Second World War (the *Epilogue* chapter gives details).

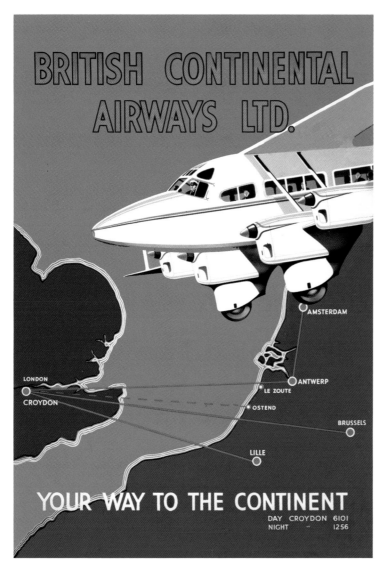

To the confusion of passengers, airlines merged, renamed or appeared and disappeared with remarkable frequency during the 1930s. British Continental Airways, whose slogan was 'The British Airline', operated for a mere 16 months during 1935 and 1936. Formed to serve Continental destinations from Croydon Airport, it operated the routes shown on this poster together with a Liverpool–Doncaster–Amsterdam service in partnership with Dutch airline KLM. Following a dispute in early 1936 it agreed to merge with British Airways Ltd.

A leisure pursuit alone?

There is a widespread impression, that during the inter-war years, flying was an elite leisure pursuit for those with expensive tastes and the wherewithal to support them. The presumption is made that air travel was the exclusive province of the well-to-do sections of society — families of wealth, film stars and the like. The notion is reinforced by newspaper reports, cinema newsreels and aspirational advertisements in magazines such as *Punch*. This is false history, however, as the academic writer Gordon Pirie has pointed out. The majority of flyers on commercial airline routes in the 1930s, his detailed research indicates, were businessmen and other passengers on work assignments. On Empire air routes people flying on commercial or personal business outnumbered leisure journeys by three to one.

Flying was certainly affordable for wealthy individuals and families but high fares put air travel out of reach of most holidaymakers in the 1930s.

Tourism came about purely incidentally and only for those flying long-distance on paid business or public service errands, in consequence of the slow, low altitude, daylight flights that stopped frequently for refuelling along the new routes to the Empire. The novelty of aerial views added to the scenic value of air travel, whilst its unpredictability added to the adventure value of flying.

The closest that most people got to flying was at air shows, where small numbers of people could join a pilot on a short joy flight (we cover this again in the chapter *Public Awareness*). A number of flying clubs were established around the country, where some fortunate individuals flew privately for pleasure in small, light aircraft. Most of these had hospitable club houses at the airfield, where friends and family would gather for congenial relaxation. Some wealthy businessmen owned private aircraft that they used for professional and leisure travel. One of these was Edward Hillman, who owned a number of bus and coach companies operating in Essex as well as Hillman's Airways, with flights to the near Continent as well as within the British Isles. Hillman was a man who enjoyed making an impression and when he expanded his fleet with a new AEC Renown luxury touring coach, he flew his own private aeroplane to the maker's works at Southall to take delivery.

Opposite: Ninety-minute flights from London to Paris at a price of six guineas return were the headline deal at the Air France counter at Croydon Airport in 1935. At this time the average weekly wage for a working man was just £5. The price of luxury items was often expressed in guineas, which were worth 21 shillings (£1.05 in decimalised currency).

Chocks away! An official signals the pilot of Imperial Airways' airliner *Heracles* to take up his take-off position, while further away another man removes the chocks from the wheels. The four-engined plane carried 38 passengers from Croydon to Paris together with a crew of five. Meals were served from the kitchen on board.

Cargo went too

Export products with a high value to weight and volume were a natural candidate for air freight, which could offer timely delivery. Some of the first customers to realise the value of air transport in the 1920s were banks and other business houses, which had bullion, diamonds or vital documents to send to or from other countries. The airlines developed this business and during the 1930s a limited amount of international air cargo entered and left Britain, such as daily newspapers and perfume (from Paris) by Air France and banknotes, precious metals, live animals and cut flowers by the Dutch national carrier KLM. The real boom in air freight came after the Second World War, however.

Air had a particular advantage for carrying livestock. In 1931 Imperial Airways announced that traffic of this kind had increased to the extent that it had to set up a special department to ensure that animals made their journeys in the minimum of time and could be fed and tended while in transit. Consignments included dogs, cats, mice, day-old chicks, pigeons, cage birds, fish in tanks, bees, turkeys, insects, small bears, lion cubs, rare zoo specimens and monkeys. As many as 2,000 day-old chicks were sent by plane from Croydon to Romania for one customer. Another notable flight carried a flying menagerie of parrots, monkeys and a bear, together with tanks of tropical fish. On another occasion a circus transported a fully-grown lion and its trainer from the Continent to London.

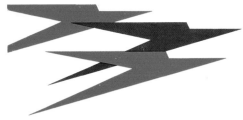

Top left: Air cargo was ably promoted by Imperial Airways, as shown by this publicity photo taken in 1931 at Croydon Airport. Being loaded is a consignment of loudspeakers from Celestion, the oldest manufacturer of these products still in business at the time of writing.

Above: Period publicity made good use of the company's 'speedbird' symbol. 'Speedbird' is still used by British Airways as a callsign during air traffic control procedures.

Left: 'Airport blight' was not an issue for residents living near Croydon Airport in 1935. Handley Page HP42E biplane *Horatius* comes in to land low enough to make passers-by stare. This Imperial Airways craft carried 24 passengers and the E suffix indicated it was designed for the company's 'Eastern' routes to India and South Africa.

BRITAIN'S PREMIER AIRPORT CROYDON

EAST COAST · WEST COAST · SCOTLAND · ISLE OF MAN · N.IRELAND · EIRE ETC:

FRANCE · GERMANY · HOLLAND · BELGIUM · SWITZERLAND · SCANDINAVIA · ITALY · ETC:

Internal Air Services

THE map below gives the towns served by air liners direct from Croydon. Railway Air Services operate services to Birmingham, Manchester, Liverpool, Isle of Man, Belfast and Glasgow. North-Eastern Airways serve the East Coast to Aberdeen, while West Coast Air Services operate via Bristol to Dublin. Other companies operating from Croydon include Air Despatch, Wrightways, Olley Air Services and Air Taxis Ltd.

Continental Services

ALMOST every town of importance can be reached from Croydon by air. The map below gives some idea of the principal services, many of them direct routes. The most important companies operating from the airport include Imperial Airways, Air France, the Deutsche Lufthansa, A.G., the K.L.M. (Dutch Air Lines), Swissair, S.A.B.E.N.A. (Belgian Air Lines), the Swedish Aerotransport Co., the Danish D.D.L., and the Avio Linee Italiane S.A.

By mid-1939 most major British cities could be reached from Croydon (further services were operated by British Airways Ltd from Heston), whilst Imperial Airways and other European national airlines served the main capitals of Europe. Passengers for Empire destinations took the train from Imperial Airways' Victoria air terminal to catch a flying boat from Southampton.

Imperial Airways recruited a modernist (and minimalist) graphic artist by the name of Theyre Lee-Elliott to design its printed publicity. As well as creating the Speedbird emblem for it together with the archetypal airmail wings for the GPO (see page 63), he also designed the envelope sticker (left) and the cover of the folder seen below.

Dated 1933 and entitled *Facts About Air Travel*, this folder sought to provide reassurance to first-time fliers. Along with advice for big game hunters, it discusses the type of clothes to wear and 'special notes on air travel for women'. It also reveals that the average passenger weighs 'not quite 12 stone' and states that because there is 'NO TIPPING many of our passengers find that they can travel to or from Africa or India with only a few shillings in their pockets without suffering any inconvenience'.

BOOKINGS

As official Agents we book for all Imperial Airways services

IA/X/69. 50m 2/33. Designs by Lee-Elliott. Printed by Lund, Humphries and published by Imperial Airways Ltd., Airways Terminus, London, S.W.1.

TIME SAVED BY IMPERIAL AIRWAYS' TRAVEL TO PLACES ALONG THE EMPIRE ROUTES

This table must be used only as a *general* guide because the savings in time may alter with variations in the services

London to:—	Time by Air	Time by Surface Travel	Time saved by Air
Athens ..	2½ days	4½ days	2 days
Baghdad ..	3½ ,,	9 ,,	5½ ,,
Karachi ..	6½ ,,	16 ,,	9½ ,,
Khartoum ..	5 ,,	8 ,,	3 ,,
Port Bell ..	6½ ,,	21 ,,	14½ ,,
Nairobi ..	7 ,,	19 ,,	12 ,,
Johannesburg ..	10 ,,	18½ ,,	8½ ,,
Cape Town ..	11 ,,	17 ,,	6 ,,

FARES ON THE EMPIRE SERVICES

Fares on the Empire routes are very little higher than the first-class fares charged by steamship companies, and in some instances are even lower. You save money as well as time by travelling on Imperial Airways' Empire services, for on these services all your meals and accommodation are included in your fare and there is NO TIPPING. In this way you have no 'extras' to pay—except your drinks and purely personal expenses—and many of our passengers find that they can travel to or from Africa or India with only a few shillings in their pockets without suffering any inconvenience

Throughout the Empire routes transport between the town and the air port, and *vice versa*, is provided by the Company wherever necessary without extra charge, and all tickets issued by Imperial Airways include the cost of this transport

The fares are based on the transport of a weight of 221 lb. (100 kg.) a passenger including luggage. The average passenger weighs 166 lb. (not quite 12 stone), and so normally 55 lb. of luggage may be taken free. If, however, the personal weight of the passenger should be 187 lb. (8½ kg.) not quite 11½ stone, or over, then 33 lb. (15 kg.) of luggage will be carried free of charge whatever the passenger's own weight may be. *Other heavy baggage may be sent in advance at cheap rates*

SOME SAMPLE FARES

N.B.—*All fares are liable to alteration without notice*
London to:—

Athens, £40 single, £54 return
Baghdad, £62 single, £111 12s. return
Karachi, £93 single, £171 return
Khartoum, £70 single, £126 return
Kampala, £105 single, £189 return
Nairobi, £109 single, £196 4s. return
Salisbury, £115 single, £207 return
Johannesburg, £125 single, £225 return
Cape Town, £130 single, £234 return

ADVICE TO THOSE TRAVELLING ON THE EMPIRE ROUTES

Imperial Airways has published a booklet entitled *Notes for your Comfort and convenience when travelling by air to India and through Africa*, and this gives all sorts of useful information about the type of clothes to wear and some precautions with respect to your health and special notes on air travel for women

EGYPT BY AIR

By Imperial Airways you can be in Cairo 2½ days after you leave London. Think of the opportunity here for Winter trips to the sun, for Spring and Autumn holidays of unusual interest

BIG GAME HUNTING

Travel by Imperial Airways brings big game shooting within the reach of many people who have been prevented from enjoying this experience from lack of time. By using Imperial Airways services you can, for example, now have a fortnight's shooting in East Africa and yet be only a month away from England

MEALS ON THE EMPIRE SERVICES

On the Empire Services all meals as well as hotel accommodation and all tips are included in the fares and are served either in the aeroplanes or flying boats or at the Company's stations

THE FLYING EXPERIENCE

The popular image of air travel was glamorous, luxurious, even decadent, to judge by press accounts, advertisements in glossy magazines, movies and newsreels. And so it was. But at the same time, flights were not always very comfortable, with airport facilities and ground transport distinctly undeveloped by today's standards. The reality is that flying was a contrasting mixture of luxury and inconvenience, both of which we shall examine now.

Particularly on international flights the standard of service was very high. Flight attendants looked after all passenger needs, whether requested or not. It is alleged, probably only in jest, that the following instructions were given to the flight attendants in the 1930s:

- Keep the clock and altimeter wound up.
- Carry a railway timetable in case the plane is grounded.
- Warn passengers against throwing their cigars and cigarettes out the windows.
- Keep an eye on passengers when they go to the lavatory to be sure they don't mistakenly go out the emergency exit.

Step on the scales please!

Air travellers of today could easily take offence at being weighed before boarding but this was absolutely normal in the 1930s. First your baggage would be weighed, with a surcharge to be paid if it was over 30lb, and then it was your turn to go on the scales. In those days it was very important to avoid overloading the plane, so a load sheet was compiled and checked before an aircraft took off. By 1939 greater subtlety was employed, at least in

A passenger weighs in at Croydon Airport in 1934 before boarding a Railway Air Services' flight to Scotland. In those days the margins between success and failure at take-off were so tight that passengers themselves had to be weighed as well as their luggage.

the magnificent new Imperial Airways' terminal in Victoria (London), where disguised scales platforms were concealed in the floor directly in front of the check-in desks. This, it was said, was because 'people of ample proportions should never be called upon to clamber aboard a weighing machine in full view of their fellow passengers'.

Fellow Travellers

Assuming that you were lucky enough to be on board a passenger flight in the 1930s, with whom might you have been sharing the accommodation? The likelihood is that you were reasonably well off as the ticket prices were not cheap. Although fares had dropped during the period — that from London to Karachi, for example, fell from £120 in 1929 to £85 a decade later (equivalent to £6,489 and £4,839 at 2013 prices) — at a time when the average wage in Britain was £209 per annum in 1938. Flying was, therefore, something that only the rich could do.

The contemporary newsreels as shown in cinemas of the period regularly featured the glamorous celebrities of the period — the famous film stars and sportsmen — travelling by aircraft. This was something that helped to foster the perceived glamour of air travel at the time. In reality, however, the majority of passengers were businessmen travelling for commercial purposes or people on government business. Many of those who took advantage of Imperial Airways' services to the far-flung reaches of the British Empire were colonial administrators and military officers either heading to or from their duties overseas.

There were tourists — big game hunters to Africa, for example, who would recoup the cost of their travel by selling trophies from the animals killed or skiers heading to Switzerland — but these were the exception and many who might have flown still preferred to take the cross-channel steamers and the railways. Overseas travel remained the province of the wealthy until the growth of the package holiday in the 1960s; for the less well off, a train or coach to a British seaside resort was the norm for the annual holiday.

Airport Security

One aspect of flying in the inter-war years that would surprise those travelling in the 21st century was the virtual lack of security at airports. In the years before World War 1, although passports did exist (and had become more sophisticated as a result of the growth of photography), the speed of land travel, particularly by train in mainland Europe, had largely rendered the concept of the border check irrelevant. World War 1 and the perceived threat of foreign agents had resulted in a revival of travel documentation and, in 1920, the newly established League of Nations held a conference in Paris on passports, customs formalities and through tickets that established a set of standards for passports issued by its member countries. The International Civil Aviation Organisation (ICAO) was established in 1947 and this body now controls passport standards.

A traveller abroad would have thus had a passport check but there were none of the security checks and screening that the modern passenger faces. Friends and relatives of passengers were, therefore, able to either greet or say farewell to passengers almost at the steps of the aircraft. Although the threat of hijacking is almost as old as civil aviation — the first recorded incident occurred in Peru in February 1931 and the first fatality involving a hijacking was in October 1939 — the actual number was relatively limited; 15, for example occurred between 1948 and 1957. However, thereafter the number grew exponentially with a peak of 82 in 1969 alone. From the late 1960s onwards, as the perceived threat level from terrorism and the international drug trade grew, so the level and sophistication of airport security increased — a far cry from the relatively relaxed environment of the era before the Second World War.

Tickets were issued but, unlike the railways where bookings were generally made in person at the station even for pre-booking, those intending to fly often made their reservations by telephone as most airlines operated their booking offices at the airports served — another element that illustrates that flying was very much aimed at the well-heeled as few, outside the middle and upper classes, would have had easy access to a telephone. Tickets generally consisted of a long series of paper coupons that detailed every leg of the trip.

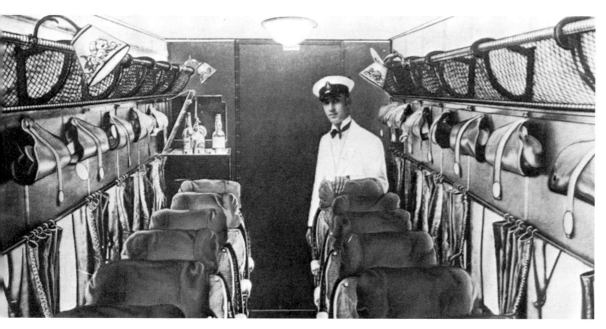

A 1927 view of the passenger cabin of the converted Imperial Airways' Armstrong Whitworth Argosy for use on the airline's luxury 'Silver Wing' service between London and Paris. This was the world's first named air service. There was room for 18 passengers, with the rearmost two seats having been removed to accommodate the bar and the steward, who served passengers a buffet lunch.

The luxury that is not expensive

So claimed Imperial Airways in an advertisement of 1932. It supported its assertion: 'The speed and luxury of travel by Imperial Airways will be a revelation to you. London to Paris in a $2^1/_2$ hours flight. To India in 7 days. To Cape Town in 11 days. In both the above Empire journeys you will sleep comfortably on land each night in accommodation provided free by Imperial Airways. There is lavatory accommodation in every Imperial Airways liner. You can book to intermediate places en route and the journey itself will be of extraordinary interest, while the time saved is of immense value. Excellent meals are served on board during flight.' Another of the company's advertising slogans was 'The Most Luxurious Travel is by Imperial Airways', which must have reassured travellers of the day, who would doubtless have been perturbed by the lack of toilets on board some other airlines' flights.

Imperial Airways in fact led the way as an innovator in creature comforts for passengers. In April 1925 it was the first airline to screen an in-flight movie to passengers, the film being The Lost World, a Hollywood silent fantasy adventure film adapted from Sir Arthur Conan Doyle's novel of the same name.

In the same vein, Imperial Airways inaugurated the world's first cooked meal on a commercial aircraft in 1927. On its London-Paris service a steward dressed in a smart white tunic serving just 18 passengers on the flight, seated in comfort more or less on a par with a railway carriage. The aircraft concerned was an Armstrong Whitworth Argosy, *City of Birmingham*, that was modified by the removal of two seats at the back — thus reducing the capacity from the usual 20 — in order to accommodate the steward and a small bar.

To complement the meal the steward had access to a small cabinet carrying four gills (quarter-pints) of whisky, a dozen bottles of lager beer, two siphons of sparkling water and 12 assorted bottles of mineral water, plus a packet of sandwiches and biscuits. The distinction of providing the first inflight meal goes, however, to Handley Page Transport, who offered pre-packed lunch boxes of sandwiches and fruit as early as 1919 on its London to Paris flights. Another innovation on the London-Paris route was the world's first airline steward, 14-year-old Jack Sanderson, who worked for Daimler Airway in 1922. His fame was short-lived, as most unfortunately he lost his life in an air crash a year later.

Passenger comfort soon became far less frugal, with increased personal space and more relaxing seats provided by the late 1930s. The Empire flying boats, which flew at 200mph, were described as offering comfortable sleeping berths, a smoking cabin and a promenade deck. Air hostesses (then called stewardesses) were an innovation of the 1930s on Air France, Swissair, KLM and Lufthansa flights but cabin service on British aircraft was provided exclusively by male stewards, who 'moved with the grace and speed of panthers' according to an American observer in 1939. This remained the case until 1943, when BOAC recruited its first stewardess, Rosamund Gilmour. Qualifications for the BOAC post included nursing experience, the ability to cook, an educated voice and infinite patience, stated the airline, but 'glamour girls are definitely not required'.

Sightseeing from the Air

The lack of pressurised cabins had little to do with technical inability but more to do with the fact that aircraft flew at a relatively low height. It was only towards the end of the 1930s that aircraft could fly at 3,000m (10,000ft). Aircraft engines of the period lacked the efficiency to be able to fly for long periods at high level and, given the relatively short distance of many of the stages, considerable fuel was expended in taking off.

There were other factors that also led passenger aircraft of the period to fly at a relatively low level. In an era before the production of aviation charts and the provision of radio beacons, pilots navigated by the identification of notable features, such as railways, on the ground that were visible only from a relatively low level. Moreover, lacking the instrumentation available to modern pilots flying in poor visibility, those of the 1930s were forced to fly below any cloud cover and aviation was severely restricted in poor weather. Sightseeing was also aided by the relatively low air speed of the aircraft; the Handley Page HP42E, for example, which was introduced in 1930 for services to India and Cape Town, had a maximum speed of 120mph and a cruising speed of 100mph.

Writers of the period noted the sights that were visible during the epic trips from, for example, London to Cape Town or to India via the Middle East. There were countless articles published in newspapers and magazines in the 1930s that extolled the sights that the airline passenger could experience and airlines such as KLM encouraged the production of books detailing what could be seen from its aircraft whilst in transit. Whilst Imperial Airways did not produce books, it did produce articles, timetables and strip maps that all identified the readily identifiable sights that passengers would see during the journey.

The Overnight Stop

Although most travellers by air during the period seem to have been businessmen, rather than tourists, those engaged in flying long-haul during the period cannot have escaped seeing the sights on land.

One of the consequences of the relatively short range of the aircraft flown on long-haul services was that frequent stops were necessary. In 1936, the Imperial Airways' timetable listed 22 journey breaks between Cairo and Cape Town. Some of these would have simply been for refuelling, but a number were overnight stops. In some of these more remote locations Imperial Airways created its own facilities that used imported food to recreate the ambience of a British hotel. In more significant places, such as Cairo, the airline used the major commercial hotels, taking the passengers from airport to hotel and back by coach.

These enforced breaks allowed the passengers to take advantage of the opportunity to make social calls or to travel to see the local sights. Those wishing to sample the nightlife, however, may have been well advised to avoid doing so, as Imperial had a policy of waking the passengers early in the morning so that the aircraft could depart at dawn with the travellers having had breakfast already.

Contrasting comforts

Early air travellers were expected to trade comfort for speed, a perception that may have lingered longer than justified. As late as July 1939 the Imperial Airways Monthly Bulletin felt compelled to reassure prospective passengers, 'There is no need to wrap yourself up. All aeroplanes are heated and air conditioned. If you do feel the need for a rug, rugs are provided — and on Empire routes, foot muffs too. These air liners are so spacious that there is plenty of room for passengers to walk about; the Imperial flying boats have a promenade deck. And there is no need to worry about noise, for the walls are insulated, allowing conversations to be carried on in a normal voice.' On Imperial Airways' flights passengers were offered complimentary hot drinks, biscuits, cocktail snacks, fresh fruit, notepaper and pencils. During the journey they could borrow playing cards, jigsaw puzzles, children's magazines and games, sunglasses, books and newspapers.

The allure of flying is something the airlines were keen to promote and the public was happy to accept. The imagery in press advertisements and publicity photographs exuded the elegance and glamour of air travel. Travellers on short-haul flights enjoyed somewhat less breathing space and physical comfort, however.

In the 1930s, unlike today, there was little to interest or amuse passengers who arrived before their flight. These people waiting in 1934 at Croydon Airport to board a Railway Air Services' flight to Scotland resorted to this cramped and spartan-looking buffet bar.

For much of the period covered by this book, there was one notable feature — compulsory in modern aircraft — that was conspicuous by its absence. Although the seat belt had been under development from the 19th century, it was only towards the late 1930s that belts started to be fitted to aircraft. In contrast, passengers flying in the period would have been able to have enjoyed a cigarette or cigar; although initially airlines were reluctant to permit smoking, pressure from the tobacco companies led to it being accepted. The glamour of aviation was used heavily during the inter-war period to promote smoking; images of well now aviation figures such as Amelia Earhart were used heavily in cigarette and tobacco advertising. It was only in the late 1980s that increasingly smoking was banned from aircraft.

For passengers the lack of toilets on some short-haul aircraft could cause discomfort, as would the turbulence and bumpy landings often mentioned in contemporary accounts. Because cabins were not pressurised in those days, ear popping could be very unpleasant for some people. Adverse weather conditions aloft could easily result in late arrival and missed connections. The journey from central London to Croydon Airport was made in a coach and took 45 minutes, whilst at some provincial airports your only option was a corporation bus (unless you prepared to pay for a taxi). To be fair, however, reserved first-class compartments were part of the offer when you flew the train from Victoria to the new Gatwick Airport in 1936. Gatwick also provided covered gangways to reach aircraft from the terminal building, but at other airports you took your chance in wind and rain. Taking the plane could be a strange blend of contrasts.

The Downside

Commercial aviation in the inter-war years was pioneering; flying itself was barely a generation old and much of the equipment used was relatively primitive. The use of hydrogen in airships such as the R101 and the *Hindenburg* had resulted in spectacular accidents and the airliners of the period were also prone to technical problems and occasional accidents. The pioneering Handley Page HP42, *Hannibal*, for example, was forced to make an emergency landing at Five Oak Green, Kent, on a flight from Croydon to Paris in August 1931 when two of its engines failed. None of the passenger or crew was, however, hurt. In 1933, in an another example, Gervas Huxley, the husband of the writer and journalist Elpseth Huxley (author of *The Flame Trees of Thika*), was stranded with fellow passengers in the bush of Northern Rhodesia for three days when the pilot of the aircraft he was on made a forced landing, having got lost and run out of fuel.

There were, however, numerous occasions when the passengers were less fortunate; in 1935 alone, for example, almost fatal 40 accidents were recorded worldwide with more than 230 deaths. Of these, the single worst accident was a Tupolev ANT-20 that crashed near Moscow killing all 50 on board the aircraft plus two on the ground. The last accident in 1935 was on New Year's Eve, when an Imperial Airways' Short Calcutta, *City of Khartoum*, came down in the sea near Alexandria having run out of fuel. One crew member survived but there were 12 fatalities. The unpredictability of air travel was also brought into sharp relief by the death or loss of many of aviation's pioneers, such Flight Lieutenant Richard Waghorn, killed in 1931 testing a Hawker Horsley biplane, Amelia Earhart, who disappeared in July 1937, and Amy Johnson, who was killed in 1941 during the Second World War when she was flying with the Air Transport Auxiliary.

The Airport of London, Croydon

At most airports passengers were expected to brave the elements, as this rather florid calendar painting of Croydon Airport shows. Fully covered gangways were, however, provided at the newer Gatwick Airport.

Powerful arguments were made for mid-city airports during the 1930s, although none was actually built. This design of 1937 would have spanned the River Thames between London's Charing Cross and Waterloo stations.

STARTLING STRUCTURES

In the 1930s newly constructed public buildings and their interior treatment offered a vivid contrast between decorous restraint (Neo-Georgian post offices, telephone exchanges, labour exchanges and similar edifices) and extreme exuberance (Odeon cinemas, zoos and the trendier hotels, factories and railway stations). With the notable exception of the austere-looking terminal building at Croydon, most airports opted for a truly contemporary appearance in the Art Moderne style. Many of them were built with public money as municipal enterprises, serving as symbols of civic pride, rivalry and modernity. Examples include the airports serving Birmingham, Liverpool, Brighton-Worthing and even places as small as Ramsgate.

The year 1936 saw the opening of the terminal building at Shoreham, where the airport was built to serve the adjacent towns of Brighton, Hove and Worthing. The building remains in use in a kind of perfect time-warp and was designated a Grade II listed building as far back as 1984.

The rather sober-looking Croydon Airport building of 1928 failed to embrace the futuristic spirit of the Machine Age. Subsequent terminals were far more adventurous in their architectural styling.

Gatwick, also opened in 1936, has the distinction of being the world's first fully integrated airport building. Both the gangways from the terminal to the aircraft and the covered approach from its railway station were fully protected from the weather, making Gatwick a nationally and internationally important example of airport terminal design. Although the structure was made obsolete by a new terminal in the 1950s, it still stands and is used as offices.

With form following function, Gatwick's 'beehive' terminal building, opened just eight years later in 1936, displays a complete contrast to Croydon. The British Airways' service van cannot match the building's sleek, attractive looks, however.

A minor gem that sadly did not survive was the municipal airport at Ramsgate, opened in 1935. Its exuberant and highly imaginative design in the Machine Age idiom took the shape of an aeroplane, with a central cockpit-style control tower and two long wings. Large expanses of glass walls styled it like a sun lounge alongside a seaside lido. Today it would be recognised as a standout period piece for its 'expressive light and grace' but it was demolished for site redevelopment in 1968.

A gloriously bijou airport was established at Ramsgate with a stunning terminal building that was actually styled to look like an aircraft. The elevated control tower represented the cockpit, whilst the tapered side extensions were the wings. When the architect David Pleydell-Bouverie designed the building he was just 26 years old; after this he emigrated to the USA and virtually abandoned architecture in favour of ranching.

City airports too

It goes without saying that all of these airports were constructed well away from built-up areas, a presumption that began to be questioned in the early 1930s. A scheme for an airport atop a giant skyscraper in New York was proposed in 1932 with the claim that 'The air passenger of the future will be rushed swiftly upward in an elevator to the flat roof of a giant building, where he will find a completely equipped aerodrome with air liners leaving for, or arriving from, all parts of the world.' The scheme's designers were convinced they could mitigate the problem of shock force effects when aircraft landed on the roofs of skyscrapers.

A year previously a more practical and fully worked-out design for a London city airport was published by the architects C. W. Glover and partners, to be built over the goods stations just north of King's Cross and St Pancras stations. The scale model exhibited in the ticket hall at Charing Cross Underground station (now renamed Embankment) revealed it would have four runways each half a mile long and 250 feet wide, all supported on a combination of new buildings and cantilever bridges.

In a Pathé film of 1933, *The Air Port of the Future*, available to view on the Britishpathe.com website, Glover explains that by providing four runways, planes can always take off or land in the direction of the wind. At night the runway in use would be illumi-

Capt. Charles Glover with a model of his London City Airport, which he proposed to construct at King's Cross.

nated, the lighting being controlled by the wind itself. Hangars for the aircraft would be provided at ground level, with lifts moving them between ground and runway levels. The cost of the project was estimated at £5 million and by relieving unemployment, it would save £2 million otherwise required from the dole fund.

The design of this novel airport attracted considerable attention on both sides of the Atlantic, making it worthwhile spending a moment to examine its ingenious features. The proposed airport was to be linked up with all forms of inland transport, as the aerodrome would be the site of an immense omnibus and long-distance motor coach garage and terminus, as well as being served also by the LMS, LNE and Underground railways. It would also be possible for freight to be distributed by means of the Regents Canal in the immediate vicinity.

Despite claims by opponents of the scheme that it would not be in the interests of public safety for aeroplanes to fly low over densely populated areas, its protagonists argued that all modern multi-engined airliners were capable of maintaining flight with one engine out of commission, and if an engine should fail after an aeroplane had taken off from the airport, it could continue its flight and make an emergency landing at Croydon or at one of the other aerodromes in the immediate vicinity of London. If engine trouble occurred over London, the pilot could decide whether he should turn and make for an aerodrome in the outskirts, or carry on and attempt a normal landing at the airport.

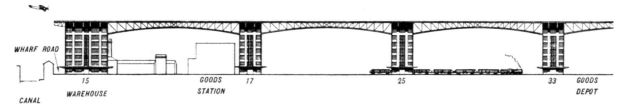

Section of one of the elevated runways intended for the London City Airport.

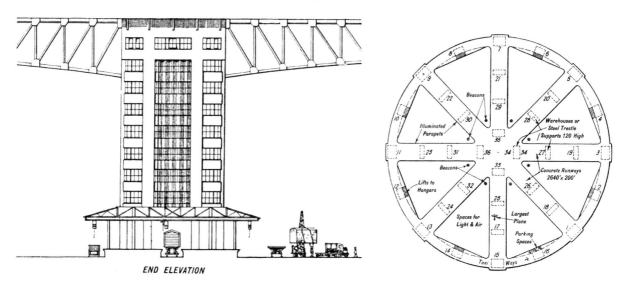

One of the pillars for supporting the elevated aerodrome, with freight transhipment facilities below.

Ground plan of the aerodrome, showing the four radial runways.

One of two impressions of how the new airport would look. This, the more artistic, provides a good feeling of the massive scale of the structure.

Opposite: A clearer and more informative view of the London City Airport planned at King's Cross. This one is from an American publication, which explains the terminology and slightly wayward geography.

Erecting the runways on elevated buildings raised them clear of all obstructions and would provide safe landing and taking-off facilities for all types of aeroplanes in all directions of wind. A machine would land on one of the runways and, after slowing down, taxi round the circular way to set down its load of passengers and mails at the main buildings. It would then travel under its own power to a parking place, or to an elevator — similar to those employed aboard aircraft carriers — that would lower it to hangars accommodated in a number, probably four, of the supporting buildings. The segmental space between the runways was to be left open in order to admit light and air to the space below. The runways were to be constructed of concrete, and to be provided with parapets along the sides to prevent machines or people from falling over.

The area selected as most suitable for the erection of the King's Cross city airport was 130 acres in extent, of which 15 acres were actually built upon. The buildings were mostly very old, however, and little difficulty was foreseen in obtaining permission to pull them down. The buildings to be erected would provide in all about 75 acres of floor space, and would be devoted to warehouses, offices, shops, flats, garages and hotel accommodation. A certain number of the buildings would be set aside as tenement-houses for people who had been dispossessed of the houses demolished. The work provided also for constructing a new road, to be known as 'Aerial Way', leading from Pentonville Road to the chief building, with a circulating area for buses and motor traffic in front of it. Also necessary was replanning the goods yards and sidings at King's Cross and realigning the main passenger line, in addition to constructing several bridges.

YORK ROAD

WIND VANES

R.R. STATION

FLOODLIGHTS

ENTRANCE TO HANGARS

ELEVATOR TO BUS STATION

RAMP TO STREET

BUS TERMINAL

ELEVATOR TO STREET

Nothing came of the King's Cross scheme nor, for that matter, of a comparable design published in 1937 that would have been built 'on stilts' above the railway bridge crossing the River Thames between Charing Cross and Waterloo stations on London (illustrated on page 28).

Rotatable runway

A weakness of the two mid-city airport schemes proposed for London (King's Cross and Charing Cross) was the space they wasted, given that only one runway could be used at any single time. A more radical design of 1937 resolved this limitation with a single-runway design on a rotatable platform, to be built above central Liverpool. The ingenious rationale was that the runway would be turned around so that aircraft could land or take off exactly against the wind.

Eight huge towers would support the runway, which was to be 1,500 to 1,800 feet long and 250 to 350 feet wide, with an enlarged central section 500 feet in diameter. The peripheral versus mid-city airport debate was relatively short-lived and petered out with the introduction of much larger aircraft whose weight these elevated structures would have been unable to take, not to mention the trickiness of take-off and landing or the perceived risk of carnage if an aeroplane failed to land safely.

Overshadowing the Three Graces beside the Mersey stands the rotary airport envisaged for Liverpool in 1937. The landing and take-off platform was to be a third of a mile in length, at a height of 320 feet to clear the fogs and ground mists that affected ground-level airports.

Convenient compromise

Having described what did not occur, we must explain what came to pass instead. Flyers expected airlines to provide a city centre to city centre journey, which was the reason for building central air terminals. Some of these were little more than a coach pickup point with an office nearby, facilities that were nothing to compare with the magnificent Empire Terminal of Imperial Airways started in 1938 and finished the following year. Designed in flamboyant Art Deco style by the architect Albert Lakeman, it was erected in Buckingham Palace Road, close to the railway and underground stations and even closer to London Coastal Coaches' Victoria Coach Station and the Green Line coach stops. It included facilities for freight and mail as well as passengers, with accommodation for airline coaches as well as taxis.

Flyers could take comfortable road coaches to Croydon Airport or a rail connection to the flying boat berth at Southampton Docks, using a direct staircase down to the private air terminal platform of Victoria station below. The striking statue over the entrance, entitled 'Speed Wings over the World', was the highest profile commission for sculptor Eric Broadbent (assisted by John W. Drake); he also executed most of the decorative work for Sir Edwin Lutyens' Britannic House in Finsbury Circus. The terminal remained in use as a check-in facility until 1980 and now forms the central block of the National Audit Office.

A late 1940s view of the BOAC (previously Imperial Airways) airline terminal in London's Buckingham Palace Road, completed just before the outbreak of the Second World War. A Commer Commando half-deck coach is entering on the left, with a Bedford OB coach emerging at the far end. Today, obsolete as a transportation facility, the main office block has been refurbished and the airport bus station on the left demolished to make room for more offices.

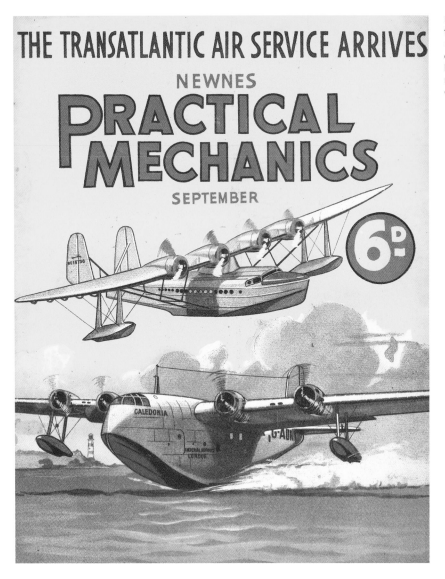

Records were broken in 1937 when the British Empire flying boat *Caledonia* (the lower of these aircraft) crossed the Atlantic in just over 15 hours. An American Sikorsky S-42 made the flight in the opposite direction.

FANTASTIC FLYING MACHINES

So rapid was the development and improvement of aircraft between 1919 and 1950 that it is easy to overlook how primitive the first passenger aeroplanes were in functionality and appearance. Given that the Wright Brothers did not even build the world's first successful aeroplane until 1903, it is remarkable that passenger air travel was a reality in Britain just 16 years later. But the progress made in the following three decades was all the more notable, as we shall see.

The starting point for powered flight was the Wright Brothers' *Flyer III* of 1905, setting a style for early aircraft in the form of low-powered biplanes made primarily of fabric-covered wood. However, in 1915 the German engineer Hugo Junkers discarded this pattern for an aircraft with an all-metal skin and a single wing with negligible external bracing. The evolution of aircraft to finely contoured, high-powered monoplanes of aluminium took less than two decades.

The biplane configuration did not become obsolete overnight by any means and new designs were still being created in the early 1930s. A biplane wing structure has a structural advantage over a monoplane at the cost of greater drag; its demise came with the quest for greater speed and the development of improved load-bearing techniques and materials.

The quest for capacity and speed

Early passenger aircraft were characterised by their diminutive size, low speed and restricted fuel capacity. All these factors constrained their ability to carry passengers, mail and freight — and thus to earn their keep. Thus we find a prestige airliner, the Armstrong Whitworth Argosy, used by Imperial Airways in launch their flagship Silver Wings service to Paris in 1927, was only a three-engined biplane carrying 18 passengers at a maximum speed of 110mph. The passengers enjoyed the appropriate seated comfort, served buffet meals by a steward, but the Captain and First Officer sat either side of an open cockpit in the nose.

In complete contrast, let's move forward eleven years and consider the same builder's 'Ensign' airliner, first flown from Croydon to Paris in October 1938 (it was ordered in 1935 but construction took longer than anticipated since constructing bombers took priority). This was the largest non-seagoing aeroplane built in Britain during the 1930s and had a range of 1,370 miles and a maximum speed of 210mph. By 1941 a total of 14 aeroplanes had been built of this 'E' class design (in which every aircraft had a name beginning with E), for Imperial Airways' European and Empire routes. Two variants were built, with 43 passengers and a crew of five carried on the European routes and 27 passengers on daytime flights (20 at night in sleeping berths) and a crew of four on the Empire routes.

Imperial Airways had a policy of naming all the craft in its fleet, following a long-established maritime tradition. Each class had its own alphabetic designation (for instance E) and within the class every member was given a name starting with the same 'class' letter — thus *Ettrick*, *Elysian* and *Endymion*. The name of the first aircraft in the class was also used as a generic description for the type overall, such as 'Ensign' class. This practice continued well into post-war days with Imperial's successor airlines BOAC and BEA.

Biplane airliners were still being built as late as 1934. This is the Short Brothers *Scylla*, which together with its twin craft *Syrinx* operated flights from London to Paris and other European cities. Its four Bristol Jupiter engines carried 39 passengers at a maximum speed of 137mph. The people in this coloured photograph are boarding at Croydon for Paris en route for South Africa.

The contrast with the airline's 'E' class monoplane, ordered just a year later in 1935, is considerable. A third longer and nearly 50 per cent faster, the Armstrong Whitworth Ensign offered increased passenger capacity and represented a step change in flying.

One of the advantages of the flying boat was its ability to take-off and land where conventional aircraft could not. Short Brother was the first company in the world to produce commercial flying boats and, in August 1928, the company's chief test pilot, John Lankester Parker, flew the prototype S8 Calcutta to Westminster for inspection by the Chancellor of the Exchequer (Winston Churchill), members of the House of Lords and others. The S8 was the first stressed skin, metal-hulled flying boat; it offered passenger accommodation to 15 although it was flown by a pilot from an open cockpit.

The flying boat phenomenon

For long-haul services over water the preferred type of aircraft was the flying boat, at least initially. The reason was economic; it had the advantage of using water to take-off and land rather than on-shore runways, which were expensive to construct. The perception of greater safety over the ocean was another factor that helped the flying boat become the basis of international airline operations in the inter-war period. The development of long-range flying boats enabled operators like Imperial Airways and Pan American Airways to open new air travel routes to British Empire destinations in Africa, Asia and Australia and across the Atlantic in the 1930s.

Two iconic designs of the 1930s were the British Short S23 'C' class Empire and the American Boeing 314 Clipper flying boats. The Empire machine was the work of aircraft manufacturer Short Brothers in response to a request from the British government in 1933 for a new long-range monoplane with adequate capacity for both passengers and air mail to be used by Imperial Airways. Imperial's Australian partner QANTAS also agreed to purchase six of these aircraft. The first entered service in 1936 and a total of 42 (including S30 and S33 variants) were constructed at Short's Rochester works. The last examples were broken up in 1947.

The Boeing Airplane Company's 314 Clipper was produced at the request of Pan American Airways in 1936, with a total of twelve built. The first of these luxurious (and massive) machines entered service in 1939 and all had been retired (scrapped or lost) by 1951. It has been noted that the standard of luxury on Pan American's Boeing 314s has rarely been matched on flights since then; the Clippers were a form of travel for the super-rich, with the return fare between New York and Southampton being comparable to a round trip aboard the supersonic aircraft *Concorde*.

Transatlantic technologies

Back in 1937 it was by no means clear which type of aircraft would provide the best solution for commercial transatlantic flight. The Empire flying boat was an obvious and proven contender but two other options were also in the frame. The second candidate was the de Havilland DH91 'Albatross' monoplane, which had then only just begun experimental flights but was eventually put into service by Imperial Airways in 1938.

Considerable interest in 1937 was focused on the Short Mayo composite aircraft, which adopted a novel approach to overcome the difficulty of launching long-range aircraft with a maximum load. Recognising that more power is required to raise an aeroplane into the air than is necessary to maintain it in level flight, the Short Mayo (nicknamed the 'pick a back plane') was two aeroplanes in one, hence the term composite. The remarkable two-in-one machine employed a large flying-boat assisting a smaller mail-plane to take off, so that the latter could be much more heavily loaded than would otherwise be possible. As soon as the required operating height was reached, the aircraft separated and the flying-boat returned to port. The upper component was a four-engined float aeroplane and it was hoped that this method would enable much larger loads of mails to be carried on the Atlantic route than by the ordinary method of ascending unaided.

One example was built, the S21 launch craft being named *Maia* (registration G-ADHK) and the S20 float-plane bearing the name *Mercury* (G-ADHJ). The combination performed successfully, making its first transatlantic flight of 2,930 miles from Ireland to Canada on 21 July 1938. No further models of this type were built, however, as improvements in-flight refuelling and the success of the de Havilland DH91 negated the attraction of the composite approach.

This Short Mayo 'composite' aircraft was the 1938 solution to the problem that aeroplanes needed more power to raise them into the air than to maintain level flight. A large flying boat assisted the smaller mail plane into the air, after which the two planes would separate, the flying boat returning to port.

The Second World War, which broke out in September 1939, produced many technical innovations in aviation, such as jet propulsion and pressurised cabins. These developments were not applied to civil aviation until the post-war period and are mentioned at the end of this book in the *Epilogue* chapter. Now, however, it's time to return to the inter-war years.

Dirigibles — dream or nightmare?

The era of the passenger airship was tragically brief, beginning with a promising future and ending just eight years later in flames and the destruction of all credibility and public confidence. In the late 1920s the airship was considered to hold many advantages over the aeroplane. It could cover considerable distances without stopping and over a five-day journey was capable of covering 7,000 miles cruising at 60mph. Aeroplanes could manage twice this speed but, if they were carrying passengers and cargo, they could not carry enough fuel to cover more than 300 miles without refuelling.

At the start of the 1930s it was far from clear which would win the Battle of the Air.

Airships were equipped with up to seven engines. They could remain aloft even if several engines failed, unlike a three-engine airliner, which could keep aloft only with difficulty if one engine failed and had to descend if two cut out. Aeroplanes suffered from engine noise and vibration, with cramped accommodation. In an airship the engines were suspended a distance below the passenger quarters, making them almost inaudible. The modern airship had room for a dance hall, a dining room, a smoking room, a lounge and a comfortable promenade, all within the envelope of the dirigible. If it had the misfortune to run out of fuel, it could still float like a balloon until it could land. The chief disadvantage was the inflammability of the hydrogen filling the envelope.

On the face of it the airship had undeniable advantages, which is why in 1924 the British government sponsored the construction of two civil airships, completed in 1929, intended for use on Empire routes. Tragically one of these, the R101, crashed on its maiden overseas voyage in October 1930, killing 48 of the 54 people on board, including its designers and the Air Minister who had initiated the programme. This disaster put paid to airship development in Britain, although the Germans pressed ahead with two sumptuously equipped airships intended to challenge giant ocean-going liners and capable of 90mph. They were the last passenger airships to be built in the period, larger than any other aircraft in terms of their length and volume. The first of the pair, LZ129 *Hindenburg*, operated a regular transatlantic service, until this too ended in disaster when it was destroyed by fire as it attempted to moor at Lakehurst (New Jersey) in 1937. On this occasion 35 people of the 97 people on board perished along with one member of the ground crew.

Both the R101 and the LZ129 had used hydrogen for buoyancy and following these accidents only helium was used. Public confidence in airships had been destroyed and there was no further development of airships for passenger transport at the time.

Autogiros and helicopters

No discussion of inter-war aircraft can ignore the development of these superficially similar aircraft, for which both civil and military roles were envisaged. Both craft use rotors but differ in the way they use them. The autogiro (pioneered in the 1920s) generates lift by using the rotor blades to alter the angle of the air as it moves upwards and backwards relative to the blades, whereas the helicopter (first developed in the 1930s) keeps aloft by pushing air downwards (forcing the rotor blades through the air).

Both fulfilled the same function, foreseen accurately by the Scottish academic and journalist Ritchie Calder in his 1934 book *The Birth of the Future*. 'I am not donning the mantle of a prophet when I speak of an aeroplane parking place in Central London,' he wrote. 'The development of the auto-gyro, which can drop on or take off from a flat roof, and the increase in its speed will supply the business man's runabout.' In this he was quite accurate, if ahead of his time, as the *Daily Mirror* newspaper building in New Fetter Lane had a rooftop helipad that saw regular use during the 1980s.

The two-seater Westland autogiro of 1935 raised comfort to a new level for this kind of aircraft. Its legs were designed to minimise the shock of unplanned or emergency 'pancake' landing.

Autogiros proved their value in Britain with the police authorities for regulating the abnormal traffic levels caused by special events such as The Derby, Boat Race and the Cup Final. However, their inability to hover in mid-air meant they lost their competitive edge to their rival, the up and coming helicopter.

The autogiro was still tagged an 'aircraft of the future' on the cover of this 1935 book based on articles from the British *Practical Mechanics* magazine.

Despite looking like a satellite dish, this circular antenna did not point skywards. Instead it was aimed at the horizon to receive microwave radio signals from a terrestrial source. Used for exchanging air traffic control messages across the English Channel, it formed part of the world's very first commercial application of microwave radio.

Installed in 1934 at Lympne (Kent), this 10ft diameter antenna was employed to direct the transmissions in a narrow, focused beam to its counterpart at Saint-Inglevert (France).

SUPPORT ACTS

To ensure that the safety of passengers and air crew was never compromised, a fascinating array of technology was employed behind the scenes. By and large this worked remarkably effectively and, whilst some of it was initially somewhat primitive, it soon grew in sophistication.

Flight control
To manage flight operations at airports elevated control rooms were used in order that flight controllers, radio (then generally called wireless) operators and management staff had visual oversight of operations. Today we would call them control towers but initially they were dubbed aerial signal cabins or boxes, partly because they performed a similar function to signal boxes on the railway and also because some (for instance the first one at Croydon) bore a remarkable resemblance to the railway structures. Close control over flying operations was crucial, with Croydon handling more than 100 arrivals and departures per 24 hours by 1939.

AERIAL SIGNAL BOX

'Aerial signal box' is the caption of this cigarette card issued in 1938. At that time some 60 scheduled flights were controlled daily from the Croydon control tower 50 feet aloft. Planes last flew from Croydon on 30 September 1959 but the control room is still there, now restored meticulously to its pre-war condition for visitors by the Croydon Airport Society.

In bad weather and at night pilots were often unable to take visual bearings. By keeping in touch by wireless telephone with land radio stations at Croydon, Pulham and Lympne, they enabled operators at those locations to telephone their bearings to the control room staff at Croydon. The latter projected the three sets of bearings on a chart using string. The point of intersection of the strings gave the position of the aeroplane at the moment of calling, enabling the pilot to be informed immediately of his position.

Control officers were in radio contact (speech and Morse code) with aircraft, plotting their position with paper flags on a huge map. A separate operator triangulated these positions using reports telephoned in from radio stations equipped with direction-finding apparatus. During the daytime pilots generally flew 'by sight', frequently following railway lines, with some of the railway stations having their names painted on the roof in large letters. At Cranbrook, 32 miles south east of Croydon and one of the highest points in Kent, the name CRANBROOK was carved out in letters in the chalk 20 feet tall. Pilots could also use radio to request calculation of their position. Visual landmarks were of no navigational benefit at night and night flying was made possible by a chain of powerful 'air lighthouses' placed strategically along the main flying routes and indicating their location with a lamp flashing in Morse code.

Back in 1921 a magazine stated: 'Croydon aerodrome's lights are visible on a clear night 30 miles away. When all the chief aerodromes are similarly equipped and the chief air routes marked by lighthouses, night flying will lose most of its dangers.' The stretch of airway between London and the Kent coast was in 1922 the first in the world to be 'scientifically illuminated', with pilots in sight of at least one of the lights throughout the whole of the journey, and at times having no fewer than three visible. The power of the beacon at Croydon was later increased to 70,000 candle power, making it visible 50 miles away and celebrated in those days. Incidentally, it appears that all the inland aerial lighthouses were dismantled and removed at the outbreak of war. The advent of radar and more sophisticated radio systems rendered them redundant and they were not replaced after the war. However, one of these beacons, from the De Havilland aerodrome at Hatfield, was saved and is a feature of the Hatfield Aerodrome History Trail in Mosquito Way, not far from its original location.

A number of airport terminal buildings carried substantial 'aerial lighthouses' on their roofs to guide in aircraft at night. The example used at Hatfield has been preserved close to it original location.

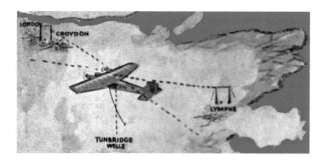

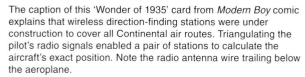

The caption of this 'Wonder of 1935' card from *Modern Boy* comic explains that wireless direction-finding stations were under construction to cover all Continental air routes. Triangulating the pilot's radio signals enabled a pair of stations to calculate the aircraft's exact position. Note the radio antenna wire trailing below the aeroplane.

By 1935 the main skyways of the world were already lit by giant beacons. On a clear night a pilot flying over Croydon at 1,000 feet could see the powerful beacon at Mont Valerien outside Paris. This collector card was given away with boys' comic *Modern Boy*.

Incidentally, the radio distress call used by aircraft and ships, 'Mayday', had its origin at Croydon Airport. According to Wikipedia, the Mayday call originated in 1923 by Frederick Mockford, who was a senior radio officer at Croydon. Mockford was asked to think of a word that would indicate distress and would easily be understood by all pilots and ground staff in an emergency. Since much of the traffic at the time was between Croydon and Le Bourget airport in Paris, he proposed the word 'Mayday' from the French *m'aidez* ('help me').

Ground support

Airport ground facilities in the 1920s and 30s ranged from the primitive to the highly sophisticated. Definitely in the former category was the 'level crossing' at the first incarnation of Croydon Airport. Opened to passenger flights on 29 March 1920, the airport had been created by 'aggregating' two small airfields that had been established on either side of Plough Lane, a public highway. To pass from one side of the aerodrome to the other, aircraft had to cross the road on the level, with a man holding a red flag to halt any road traffic. Proper crossing gates were added subsequently but within a few years this inconvenience was eliminated by closing part of Plough Lane altogether. Equally low-tech (but evidently effective) was the look-out man stationed in the 1930s on the roof of Croydon's control tower. His task was to give pilots the take-off signal, hanging a large plate bearing the machine's registration mark over the balcony and shining a powerful white lamp to guide the pilot.

Croydon Airport's rooftop look-out man used this searchlight to give pilots the take-off signal and guide them to their landing places at night.

Smiths Industries made a giant version of their well-known kitchen clocks so that pilots could check their watches from the air. The 15-foot diameter monster was installed in 1933 at Heston Aerodrome.

An imaginative innovation in 1933 was the 'giant clock' provided at Heston Aerodrome so that aircraft pilots could know at a glance whether they were on schedule or late. The 15-foot diameter clock, designed to be visible from 1,500 feet, was placed immediately in front of the control tower and illuminated by night so that it would be usable 24 hours a day.

More technology
Much higher tech and genuinely ground-breaking was the world's first commercial use of microwave radio, introduced in 1934 for controlling cross-channel air traffic. A joint venture of the British and French air

This rather primitive but effective fuelling facility was adequate at Heston Aerodrome in the early 1930s.

ministries, the system provided direct communication by teleprinter between the aerodromes at Lympne (near Hythe in Kent, about seven miles west of Folkestone) and Saint-Inglevert (35 miles away, between Calais and Boulogne, France). The technology proved highly satisfactory and led to valuable technical discoveries of how radio waves behaved at these ultra-short wave frequencies outside the laboratory. At the time, the term 'microwave' had not yet come into use and people instead spoke of 'micro-rays' and 'dwarf wave radio'.

Aircraft fuelling started off in a relatively primitive way, using larger versions of the petrol pumps seen at roadside filling stations. By the late 1930s motorised fuel tenders were in use at all main airports, with in-flight refuelling provided for transatlantic air mail clippers (page 62).

A HAWKER "HART" TAKES IN FUEL FROM A SIX-WHEELED TENDER

Although the Hawker Hart was not a civil aircraft, this period illustration is too good to waste, demonstrating as it does how aircraft were refuelled.

In 1938 the proposed George Bennie Railplane was claimed to be the ideal means of taking air passengers from central London to its airports in a reasonable time. Frequent departures combined with a six-minute journey time between Gatwick and central London theoretically provided the benefits of a central metropolitan airport.

FLYING BY TRAIN AND BUS

A major irony, of which airline operators were well aware, was the contrast between the rapidity of air travel and the slow journey to the airport. The railways might not be able to match the speed of flight, but they offered the convenience of direct travel from city centre to city centre. Airlines were expected to provide comfortable transport for passengers and their luggage to airports located outside cities, all at no extra charge. The solution, as we shall see, was to use airport buses but the rail links also offered a solution, whilst some even more radical schemes were proposed.

Trains in the air

The most novel of these rapid transit schemes was the Bennie Railplane, a remarkable hybrid of monorail and aeroplane. Scotsman George Bennie's creation envisaged a streamlined single carriage, suspended from an overhead rail and guided by another rail below the 'railplane'. It was to be driven by engines and airscrews at either end, with predicted speeds of 120mph. At this velocity, it was claimed, a lifting action similar to that of an aeroplane came into play that diminished frictional losses by reducing pressure on the rails. Ball and roller bearing devices were also used to reduce friction to 5lb per ton of load, so that speeds of 120mph on the level would require just 120hp of drive. The type of trestle construction envisaged was said to reduce the cost of constructing the engineering works, which could span large stretches of water with ease and negotiate gradients more severe than on conventional railways.

Two double-track lines were proposed, running out to airports from central London above existing railway lines for most of the way. The first would run from Holborn Viaduct to Croydon airport and the other from Paddington to Heston Aerodrome, with six-minute journey times claimed. According to its promoters the cost of constructing and operating a railplane route was significantly less than for conventional railways and would generate a profit with as few as three passengers aboard. Air journey time could also be saved by providing passport and customs examination on board the railplane.

Unlike some of the futuristic schemes described in this book, Bennie's railplane was constructed, albeit only in the form of a short demonstration line. This was built at Milngavie, north-west of Glasgow, in 1929 and later partly demolished in 1941 to assist the scrap metal campaign, although the railplane survived until 1956. The two lines to London's airport never came to pass, however, and Bennie himself was declared bankrupt in 1937, after failing to secure funding for further development of his dream.

World's first rail-air link

Britain's railway companies, as we have already seen, took a keen interest in air travel. They set up their own airline, Railway Air Services, and invested in certain other airlines. They operated other kinds of alliance too, such as their support for the flying boat services operated by Imperial Airways from Southampton. These flights began operation in 1937 to Alexandria and South Africa, initially using a pontoon in the Western Docks. A dedicated mooring and terminal were built the following year. Initially passengers took a normal express train to Southampton but after the new Airways Terminal at Victoria opened in 1939 special trains ran to Southampton Terminus from newly opened facilities on platform 17 at Victoria station. The train included a Pullman car in which passengers took meals and this direct rail-air link was described as the first in the world in which travellers took a private train from a private station attached to an air terminal.

A special platform for air travellers was constructed below the Airways Terminal at Victoria. This is the first Imperial Airways' special train about to take passengers to Southampton Docks, where they would board a flying boat on 6 June 1939. The locomotive carries a headboard with triple 'Speedbird' motifs and the words Imperial Airways Special Train.

The Airways Terminal was built almost opposite Victoria Coach Station (opened in 1932) in Buckingham Palace Road and was brought into use on 5 June 1939 (replacing a smaller office near Victoria station). The terminal was built with direct passenger access to platform 17 (now platform 19) of the railway station, a separate goods tunnel and a lift were provided for luggage or freight to be brought by small trucks and placed aboard trains. At the time a magazine enthused over the new facilities for air passengers at Victoria saying: 'This station has every modern equipment in the way of waiting halls, refreshment facilities, luggage handling apparatus, and so on.'

The pre-war Gatwick Airport station building, seen here in 1956 two years before it was replaced by the current airport station, was constructed in the 'art moderne' style favoured in the mid-1930s, although the utilitarian footbridge and platform canopies were in no way stylish. For travellers' convenience, particularly in inclement weather, a subway ran from the station forecourt direct into the airport's terminal building.

Special stations for airports

Another initiative of the Southern Railway encouraged travellers to 'take the plane to catch the train', to use a more recently coined slogan. Special airport stations were provided for Gatwick and Shoreham airports, whilst another was built but never opened at Lullingstone (as discussed in the chapter on *Flights of Fancy*). The railway facilities at Shoreham hardly matched the stylish 'art moderne' terminal building and were no more than a pair of wooden platforms with hut-like passenger shelters. They were at least located close by the terminal building, which enabled the railway to rename this existing halt Shoreham Airport in 1935. This qualified it as the first airport station in Britain. The structure established at Gatwick in 1935 was far more worthy, built in a 'art moderne' style that would have made a good match with the architecture of Shoreham's terminal building (but ironically not with Gatwick's). The station building was built in red brick, which clashed with the white concrete of Gatwick's Beehive terminal building. Bizarrely it opened with the name Tinsley Green (for Gatwick Airport) but sense prevailed and within a year it was renamed simply Gatwick Airport. It remained in use until 1958, when the present Gatwick Airport station opened.

Airport coaches

No other airports of the inter-war era enjoyed the good fortune of having their own railway station and had instead to rely on road services. For Croydon, which opened in 1920 as London's first airport, these were fraught with some difficulty. The original location was not easy to reach by road, since the Croydon Bypass, now known as Purley Way, was not built until April 1925 and there were no local buses passing the location. This was rectified in due course, however.

In the early days of air travel, when aeroplanes carried only a few passengers, it was easy enough to transport travellers in large cars, of the type then called shooting brakes and now known as people carriers. Bus-size vehicles were not required in those days but once flying developed, airlines found themselves needing to accommodate 20 or more people at a time. This was the time that they turned to single-deck buses or coaches equipped with 25 or 32 seats that were often provided at the rear with a secure compartment for mail and valuable cargo as well as passengers' luggage. In London these were generally built on AEC Regal or Leyland Tiger chassis and were operated by contractors such as Thomas Tilling. The journey from Victoria to Croydon Airport took 45 minutes during the mid-thirties.

Outside London many of the airports were operated by local authorities, which in many cases also ran local bus services. In these cases it was normally corporation buses that ran to and from the airport.

Back in 1927 passengers for the Continent flying by Imperial Airways took this 'motor car' from the airline's Charles Street headquarters in fashionable Mayfair to 'whisk them to Croydon air-station' as the period caption stated.

USE THE
AIR MAIL
THE FASTEST MAIL

A 1933 GPO poster promoting air mail services, featuring the then-new Royal Mail-branded Armstrong Whitworth AW15 Atalanta airliner that was developed for Imperial Airways' South African and Far Eastern routes.

The design was by well-known poster artist Frank Newbould, whose work was used widely by railway companies, the Empire Marketing Board and the War Office. However, the poster did not appeal to the Traffic Manager of Imperial Airways, Dennis Handover, who considered it 'not nearly up to some of his other efforts'. In this he was not wrong.

MAILS BY AIR

Most people would be surprised to learn that air mail in Britain is over a century old, the first instance dating back to September 1911, when a pilot by the name of Gustav Hamel carried mails on a 21-mile flight from Hendon (north-west London) to Windsor in a Blériot monoplane. Hamel's payload was postcards commemorating the coronation of King George V, intended for delivery to the king himself, who had given permission for the aeroplanes to land in the grounds of Windsor Castle. A local newspaper, the *Windsor, Slough and Eton Express*, reported in its Saturday 16 September 1911 edition rather prophetically: 'The Aerial Post has been the chief topic of the week. Success attended its inauguration but it is not likely to become a permanent institution yet awhile.' In similar vein it continued, 'Some splendid flights have been made to and from Windsor, and it is conceivable that one day there will be a flying department of our Post Office. ... The service is too costly yet for regular use, and it is also too risky. It is hoped, however, that something more than passing interest will be taken in this latest endeavour to keep abreast of the times.'

This exploit is legitimately celebrated as the first scheduled air mail service, authorised as such by the Postmaster General, but it is only fair to record that it was discontinued after six days and in reality no more than a historical curiosity. Serious use of aeroplanes to carry mails began immediately after the Armistice in November 1918, when the Royal Air Force and military authorities organised an experimental air mail facility between Folkestone and Cologne that operated between December 1918 and the summer of 1919. Established to provide British Army troops stationed in Germany with a rapid mail service, its success demonstrated the opportunities offered by the aeroplane for the faster carriage of mails. At the same time, the RAF was also operating a mail (and passenger) service for delegates from London attending the Peace Conference in Paris. This service ended in August 1919 but the precedent was soon followed by the establishment of a public GPO London–Paris air mail service on 10 November, 1919. The service was extended to The Netherlands, Belgium and Morocco the following year. If the take-up was not breathtaking, the charge of 2s 6d an ounce may have been the reason (by 1935 the rate was just 2d an ounce to Europe and just 1½d for Empire air mails).

Air Mail expands

When Alcock and Brown completed their pioneering non-stop flight across the Atlantic on 14 June 1919, they also carried with them 196 items of mail. Later the same year the first air mail was carried from England to Australia although in contrast to the London–Paris service, neither of these exploits was an official public facility. By the early 1930s the Post Office had established regular overseas mail services to Europe and some colonies. These were operated by Imperial Airways from Croydon Airport, the airport closest to London at the time, and by 1936 letters from the UK could be sent by air mail to more than 100 countries overseas.

A major initiative was the Empire Air Mail Scheme, under which all first class mail to destinations throughout the British Empire was to be carried at a rate of one and a half pence per half ounce, with a charge of one penny for postcards. Imperial Airways was engaged to carry mail by air on routes served by the airline. The scheme began on 28 June 1937, when the flying boat *Centurion* flew from Southampton to South Africa. The second stage, to India and Malaya, began in February 1938 and the third stage to Australia in July 1938. The service rapidly came to play an important part in the life of the Empire by 'facilitating personal and business communications between the Mother Country and the various Dominions and Colonies'. By 1939 more than 40 million items of air mail were being handled annually at Croydon.

Inland air mail began in 1934, when the first air mail flights were made between points within the United Kingdom. Known as the town-to-town service, this served major centres such as London, Birmingham, Manchester, Liverpool, Cardiff, Belfast and Glasgow. Introduced on an experimental basis, it lasted until withdrawal as a result of war.

Distinctive blue pillar boxes were provided in many cities and towns for air mail; the first eleven of these were established in what were called 'prestige locations' during June 1930. The original notion was that providing separate blue boxes for air mail would speed the sorting of the post but after 1937, when all post to the Empire and European countries was carried by air at surface

In June 1930 eleven special air mail pillar boxes, painted bright blue, were introduced to the streets of London and by 1936 their number had risen to 139 in London and 174 in the provinces. This example stood outside the General Post Office in King Edward Street, London from 1930 to 1939.

rates, the need for separate air mail posting boxes effectively vanished. Beginning in August 1938 the blue posting boxes were withdrawn, the last to go being the first to be provided (outside the General Post Office in King Edward Street, London EC1). However, a preserved example has been erected in Windsor at the junction of the High Street and St Albans Street.

The New World too

Transatlantic air mail took off in 1939, when the US Post Office Department awarded a foreign air mail (FAM) contract to Pan American Airways for two routes east across the Atlantic Ocean to Europe. One of these, the FAM-18 Northern route, flew via Canada, Newfoundland and Foynes (Ireland) to Southampton. It was inaugurated on 24 June 1939, flown by a Boeing 314 Clipper flying boat. To help promote use of this service, Imperial Airways participated with Pan American Airways in providing a special 'around the world' service to carry souvenir mail. Imperial carried mail from New York forward from Foynes to Hong Kong, from where Pan American took it on to San Francisco, with United Airlines handling the final flight to New York, arriving on 28 July.

Not to be outdone, the GPO's own British North Atlantic Air Mail Service was inaugurated on 5 August 1939 when the flying boat *Caribou* of Imperial Airways left Foynes for New York. Only eight round trips were completed before war broke out, at which time the Empire and European schemes were suspended. Many services were established again once arrangements for censorship were introduced. Full air mail services were restored again after the war, beginning in 1948.

In 1937 the Royal Mail inaugurated inland air mail services to the Orkney and Shetland Islands, replacing the 16-hour sea voyage by a 135-minute flight. The illustration is from a cigarette card issued in 1938.

To raise the profile of its new 'Royal Air Mail Service' the Post Office introduced a strikingly streamlined collection and delivery van for publicity purposes. Its dorsal fin body, designed by Maurice Lambert, was constructed on a standard 15cwt van chassis.

A special blue livery differentiated the streamlined air mail van. The same distinctive colour was used for air mail pillar boxes in the street. Toy replicas of both were included in the pre-war Dinky Toys range. The Royal Mail Air Service Car (model 34a) now fetches three-figure sums and the air mail pillar box (12b) is also highly collectible.

Mail planes

During the pre-war era most aircraft did not have the power to combine carrying cargoes with their primary passenger-carrying role, which is why some craft were built exclusively for carrying mail. One of these, designed as a dedicated transatlantic mail carrier, was the four-engined de Havilland DH91 Albatross. Seven of these were built for Imperial Airways in 1938–1939, two as mail planes and the remaining five as passenger craft.

The flying boats used on Empire routes were normally able to cope with the modest volume of letters to their destinations, although at Christmas and the New Year the peak levels of seasonal greetings demanded alternative solutions. In 1938 for instance, the 'pick-a-back' composite craft combination of *Maia* and *Mercury* was pressed into service, with the latter aeroplane making two flights carrying Christmas mails to Alexandria. This was, however, only an experiment and was not repeated. The two transatlantic services introduced in 1939 employed larger flying boats. Pan American used Boeing 314s on the FAM-18 Northern route, whilst Imperial Airways deployed Short Brothers S30 craft on the British North Atlantic service.

With a massive wing span of 152 feet and a mail and cargo payload of 10,000lb, the Boeing Airplane Company's 314 Clipper was one of the largest aircraft of its time. Its cruising speed of 188mph at 11,000 feet and range of 3,685 miles gave it range necessary for flights across the Atlantic and Pacific Oceans. Twelve of

Imperial Airways' de Havilland DH91
Albatross machine was designed for
carrying mails across the Atlantic. This
particular example, *Fortuna*, seen here at
Croydon Airport in 1939, was a 22-seater
passenger craft; the mail versions had fewer
windows.

the Boeing 314 and the improved 314A; nine were sold to Pam Am and three, in 1941, to BOAC after the latter's own transoceanic flying boats had been requisitioned by the RAF. The S30 machines *Cabot, Caribou, Clyde* and *Connemara* used by Imperial Airways were less well endowed than PanAm's Clippers, with a payload of 4,270lb and a range of over 2,500 miles, a consequence of being fitted with in-flight refuelling equipment and extra fuel tanks for use on the transatlantic airmail service. Cruising speed was 163mph and maximum height 20,000 feet.

Nearly a ton of the Christmas mails were loaded aboard the Mayo composite aircraft *Mercury* in 1938. Launched into the air by the flying boat *Maia*, a couple of non-stop flights were made to Alexandria (Egypt) from Southampton Water.

BY AIR MAIL
PAR AVION

Right: The Pan American World Airways Boeing 314 *Yankee Clipper*, circa 1939. This aircraft started the transatlantic mail service.

Left: The British North Atlantic air mail service used Short S30 class flying boats, of which *Connemara* was one. Here she is seen on the River Medway close to her birthplace at Rochester Seaplane Works.

Death-defying feats of airmanship thrilled the public during the 1920s and 1930s. They were a major feature of both RAF flying displays and also outdoor entertainments run by freelance 'operators such as Alan Cobham's Flying Circus' and lesser imitators.

PUBLIC AWARENESS

Many commentators have named the inter-war period (the 1920s and 1930s) the 'golden age' of aviation, not for the number of people travelling by air but for its remarkably potent appeal in popular and political symbolism. Put another way, although air travel between the wars was the province of the elite well-to-do, it was not cloaked in exclusive obscurity. Flying had a fascination for young and old; it represented simultaneously the future and a means of escape from the ordinary. With public awareness so high, it took little time for flying to touch most people's lives in one way or another, even if only as an experience shared in novels and cinema or at air displays.

The silver screen

Films depicting the world of the future were popular in the late 1920s and numerous futuristic aeroplanes fly over the dystopian city in *Metropolis* (Germany, 1927, set in the year 2026) and over London in *High Treason* (UK, 1929, a vision of 1940). Possibly the first airborne disaster movie (in fact a comedy of sorts) was the almost forgotten *Madam Satan* (1930), part of which was set aboard a dirigible airship that was struck by lightning (by all accounts the special effects were fairly successful). More genuinely dramatic was the mid-Atlantic seadrome stricken by sabotage that was the focal point of the film *F.P.1* (Germany, 1932), which was released in English, French and German language versions. Hans Albers starred as the heroic aviator Ellisen in the film.

Autogiros gave a touch of topicality or modernity to a number of films of the 1930s, for instance in Hitchcock's 1935 film *The 39 Steps*, enabling the reluctant hero Richard Hannay to escape from the police. The classic science fiction film *Things to Come* (UK, 1936) sees the heroes of the story travel in an autogiro, which

The impressive floating platform of the 1933 film *F. P. 1* (made simultaneously in English, French and German versions) was purely fictional. Nevertheless the concept of 'seadromes' for refuelling and servicing planes in mid-ocean remained a very real project for two decades.

Imaginative derring-do, 1937 style. By this time the notion of transatlantic air travel was not far off becoming reality.

must have been considered still sufficiently futuristic for the year in which this part of the film is set, 2036. Most of the action of the murder thriller *Non-Stop New York* (UK, 1937) is set aboard a transatlantic flight from London to New York, whilst *Sherlock Holmes in Washington* (USA, 1943) also portrays direct flight between the two capitals as current reality for the time rather than a yet unfulfilled dream.

Air fairs and flying displays

Flying displays were a major spectator sport in the 1920s and 30s and none was greater than the Pageants and Displays organised by the Royal Air Force at Hendon, north-west London. From 1920 to 1937 vast crowds arrived by bus, Underground and other means to witness what have been described as the 'greatest exhibitions of military aviation in the world' (20,000 seats were set out, 160,000 admission tickets printed and parking provided for 7,000 cars). Those unable to attend saw the displays and mock aerial battles in the newsreels at the cinema.

Other air displays were held during this period around the country, at Brooklands flying school and main RAF airfields (on Empire Air Day for instance) as well as the International Air Rally at Lympne (Kent), which promised visitors would see the RAF Hendon aerobatics team, racing and live parachuting.

Also very popular were air races, such as the Schneider Trophy and King's Cup contests. Crowds of more than 200,000 spectators attended these races, which were effectively speed contests for seaplanes. The 1929 and 1931 events were held on the Solent and both were won by British contestants flying at over 300mph. The King's Cup Race, an annual cross-country contest for aviators was Britain's premier air event, run from 1922 to 1938 and resumed after the war. Generally the event finished at Hatfield, Brooklands or Hendon, where the winner would receive the cup originally presented by King George V.

Left: A 1927 poster issued by the Underground for one of the annual RAF displays at Hendon Aerodrome held between 1920 and 1937.

Below left: 1930 as they return to Colindale Underground station from the RAF air pageant held at the nearby Hendon Aerodrome. Every year from 1920 to 1937 up to 160,000 people thronged to Hendon to attend these flying displays. The site is now home to the RAF Museum.

Below: Clarity, simplicity and style come together in this poster from June 1934 for the final of the King's Cup air race. Hatfield Aerodrome is illustrated on the cover of this book.

Less formal events were just as popular with the public. Several new airport openings were marked with air fairs arranged to attract publicity, whilst people could view flying circuses or take a joy flight provided by itinerant operators. The term 'flying circus', coined during the First World War by British pilots, related originally to large formations of German fighters, such as the one led by Manfred von Richthofen, the Red Baron. Our boys called them circuses, not only on account of their brightly painted aircraft but also because of the teams' high level of mobility from living in tents that could be relocated rapidly to a new theatre of conflict. After the war the name was transferred to travelling air displays that toured the country, performing death-defying aerobatics, wing walking and other stunts.

A major event of 1929 was a five-month aerial tour throughout Britain organised by Sir Alan Cobham in a campaign to convince local authorities of the need for municipal airports. This, states air historian John Viner, was a tour of heroic proportions in which 3,500 mayors and councillors and 10,000 schoolchildren were given free flights, sponsored by Lord Wakefield, founder of Castrol oils and a Methodist philanthropist. Some 250,000 other joy flights were made by members of the public during this tour.

Heroes (and heroines) of the air

Something else that must be mentioned is the heroic status accorded to aviators during the 1920s and 1930s. No doubt the daring of the flying aces of First World War had something to do with this and the newspapers and newsreels certainly lionised the epic exploits of the pioneering aviators. British aviators Alcock and Brown achieved unique honour (and knighthoods) by making the first non-stop transatlantic flight in 1919, whilst American Charles Lindbergh achieved worldwide fame in 1927 with his solo non-stop flight from New York to Paris (nearly 3,600 miles or 5,800 km), in a single-seat, single-engine plane the *Spirit of St Louis*.

The famous Scottish pioneer aviator Jim Mollison achieved fame by flying from Australia to England in eight days, 19 hours (1931) and from England to South Africa in four days, 17 hours (1932). Equally noteworthy were Amy Johnson (in 1930 the first woman to make a solo flight from England to Australia) and Amelia Earhart (in 1932 the first female to fly the Atlantic solo, who disappeared over the Pacific Ocean in 1937).

Regularly in the news too were the air racers, such as Flight Lieutenant Richard Waghorn, who flew the winning aircraft in the 1929 Schneider Trophy seaplane race and then continued with experimental and high speed flying until his untimely death following a crash in 1931.

Famous flier 1: Jean Batten astonished the aviation world breaking the record flying time from Australia to England.

"TURF" CIGARETTES

1929 Won Schneider Trophy Race
328.63 m.p.h. at Calshot
Supermarine S.6

F/O H. R. D. WAGHORN

50 FAMOUS BRITISH FLIERS Nº 24

Famous flier 2: Flying Officer Waghorn was another of the flying aces celebrated on cigarette cards during the inter-war years.

In 1928 another famous flier was Captain Gordon Olley, who flew the biplane *City of Glasgow* when Imperial Airways challenged the London and North Eastern Railway's 'Flying Scotsman' service to a race over the London to Edinburgh journey. Although the pilot confused the 'Scotsman' with another train near Berwick, he still managed to arrive in Edinburgh first. The photo shows the start of the race at King's Cross station in London.

More image making

Aerial extravaganzas were a firm favourite of cinema newsreels and audiences besotted with anything aeronautical. Cameras covered numerous air shows, airport openings and new aircraft, whilst BBC Television got in on the act when it sent an outside broadcast unit to cover an air race starting from Hatfield in 1937. BBC TV cameras and the cinema newsreels both covered Prime Minister Neville Chamberlain's return from his meeting with the Nazi leaders to Heston Aerodrome on 16 September 1938 holding up his famous piece of paper from Mr Hitler ('Peace in our time').

An ingenious publicity stunt was a 'plane versus train' race on 15 June 1928 when Imperial Airways' Argosy airliner G-EBLF *City of Glasgow* carrying 18 passengers from Croydon to Edinburgh (Turnhouse) challenged the London & North Eastern Railway's crack 'Flying Scotsman' express to a race. Despite having to make two stops for refuelling, the airliner completed the journey about 15 minutes faster.

Advertisers were also very conscious of the power of air travel and aviation. Imperial Airways were happy to allow Shell to share the glory of its achievements, with Shell very aware that motorists would be keen to put the 'right stuff' in their cars' petrol tanks. Amy Johnson, the first female pilot to fly solo from Britain to Australia, was happy to accept sponsorship from advertisers. On this trip, when she reached Karachi, large newspaper advertisements proclaimed: 'Am delighted with the Wakefield Organization and Castrol XXL Motor Oil gave magnificent and faultless lubrication—Amy Johnson.'

The Imperial Airways flying boat "Centaurus" has flown from New Zealand to Sydney. This is the first time that a commercial flying boat has made this trip. Shell is glad to have shared in this historic event by supplying both the petrol and the lubricating oil.

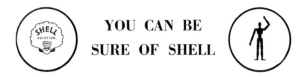

Topical tie-in advertising relying on public awareness of flying feats was considered worthwhile in 1938.

The AA's own air arm

Another organisation that used aviation to increase public awareness was the Automobile Association, which employed an airship for road traffic spotting during the 1920s. Beginning in 1928 it also used two light aircraft to deliver messages (and possibly also small car components) by throwing them out in a flagged canister to a waiting patrolman. The AA has always been first and foremost an assistance service for motorists but it used to provide similar facilities for flyers as well. In the late 1920s some AA members were joining flying clubs or even buying their own planes, leading the AA to form an aviation section in 1929, initially to survey landing grounds and provide information about changes or obstructions.

In 1932 the AA's aviation services was operating two light aircraft to support its pilot members. The registration letters G-AAAA on this De Havilland 'Puss Moth' were registered to Mr Ivor McClure, who headed the AA's Aviation Department.

In fact the aviation department expanded so rapidly that when the Schneider Trophy air race took place over the Solent, the Association was able to provide air scouts on the adjacent landing field to assist the hundreds of visiting pilots coming from all over Europe. Maps and information were being supplied to pilot members and soon international flying permits were being issued as well. From 1931 to 1933 (when the Air Ministry assumed the role), the AA transmitted radio weather reports every hour from Heston Aerodrome for the benefit of pilots.

The AA produced the first air-route maps and was the first to supplement telephone and post by dropping messages to patrols from aircraft. The famous aviator Amy Johnson worked with the AA to plan her 1932 World Record flight to Cape Town in a De Havilland 'Puss Moth' and pioneer aviators such as her one-time husband Jim Mollison benefited from the AA's information on foreign air regulations and the state of landing fields overseas.

The AA aviation section continued until the outbreak of the Second World War.

Skywriting and advertising

Advertising and flying were also linked in the public eye by skywriting and planes towing advertising banners, particularly at the seaside. Both techniques were popular during the inter-war years and companies that still offer aerial banners assert that these messages demand attention, and when one appears overhead people gaze instinctively with curiosity. Even more effective is skywriting, a process in which a small aircraft emits special smoke during flight and flies in special patterns to create writing readable from the ground. The first use of skywriting for advertising purposes was in 1922. It is no longer seen in Britain, having been made illegal by the Aerial Advertising Act of 1983.

L'Hydravion des Routes d'Empire – 28 en cours de construction
26 m. 80 de longueur • hauteur à partir de la ligne de flottaison 7 m. 30
Vitesse 320 • envergure 35 m. • Poids de charge environ 18 tonnes

IMPERIAL AIRWAYS
L'EUROPE • L'AFRIQUE • LES INDES • L'EXTRÊME ORIENT • L'AUSTRALIE

Poster advertising and branding on brochures for air travel (and air mail services) varied between the mundane and the sublime. Imperial Airways' early posters were somewhat staid but before long they matched the artistic and graphic quality of the best commercial posters of their period. The much imitated but never surpassed 'speedbird' symbol gave Imperial's publicity a distinctive look that set it apart from British Airways Ltd, Railway Air Services and other lesser airlines. Some examples of branding are given on the next page.

Imperial Airways followed the lead of organisations like Shell and London Transport in their use of strong graphic and architectural design. The speedbird motif was designed for the airline in 1932 by the artist Theyre Lee-Elliott to represent speed, flight and power.

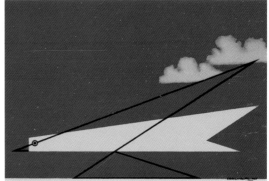

Above: This rather less inspiring avian creature was designed by Edward McKnight Kauffer for promoting the Post Office air mail service in 1935.

Left: This image was designed around 1938 for British Airways Ltd by Theyre Lee-Elliott, the same artist who created the Speedbird motif for Imperial Airways Ltd with rather greater impact.

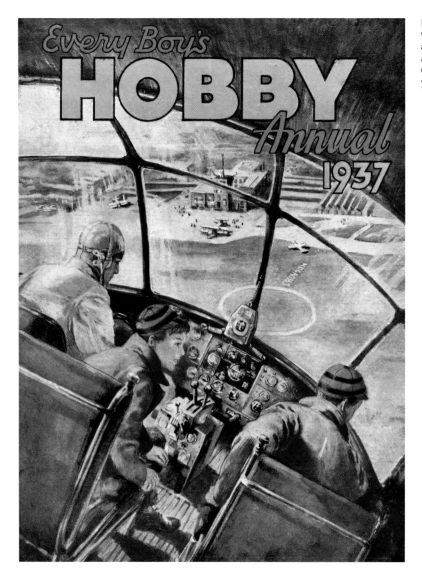

In the 1920s and 1930s just about every boy was obsessed with flying, whilst there were also many air enthusiasts of a more mature age. Sitting with the pilot, flying over Croydon Airport, would have been every youngster's dream in 1937.

POPULAR PASTIMES

'The boy of today can make a wonderful hobby of aeroplanes,' declared an unnamed writer in *Every Boy's Hobby Annual* for 1928. 'He can, at little cost, make and fly models; he can study types, engines and new inventions; he can put his thinking cap on and try to discover something new and useful in the flying of his models; he can study aeroplane parts, so that the machines become as familiar to him as his bicycle.' Taking up this theme, we examine some aviation-related hobby activities of the golden age of flying.

Spotters' delight
Aircraft spotting was a natural pursuit for those who lived near an airport or could make a special visit. Several books and boys' comics made the task easier by illustrating silhouettes of well-known aircraft and providing other recognition details. Although identifying and recording aeroplanes might have appeared a trivial pursuit, it created a dedicated army of highly skilled volunteer observers who came into their own when war broke out in 1939.

Croydon Airport was a great location in the 1930s for spotting aircraft arriving from far and near. See how many of these airline insignia you can recognise...

1. British civil air ensign; 1a. Imperial Airways (design on nose); 2. Air France; 2a. emblem on side of Air France aircraft; 3. Deutsche Lufthansa; 3a. Tail marking on all German aircraft; 4. KLM Royal Dutch Airlines; 4a. Markings on nose; 5. Railway Air Services (on fin); 5a. stripes on fuselage; 6. Tail marking for all Swiss aircraft; 6a. Swissair (nose marking); 7. Belgian Airlines (SABENA); 8. Swedish Air Lines; 9. Denmark (DDL); 10. Avio Linee Italiane (Italy). Mail-carrying aircraft carry a special official emblem on the fuselages; British-registered aircraft sometimes fly a special pennant (a blue triangular flag with a crowned bugle emblem in yellow and the legend ROYAL AIR MAIL in white) as well.

AIRCRAFT
The De Havilland "Frobisher" class. Top speed, 234 m.p.h.; 22 seats; 2,100 h.p. on four engines. Operates from Croydon with the A.W. "Ensigns" over most of the European routes.

D.H. "Dragon Rapide." Extensively used on many internal air routes. Speed, 157 m.p.h.; seats, 10. Above machine owned by Wrightways Ltd., who operate freight service to Paris.

D.H. "86 B." Ten passenger, 166 m.p.h. air liner used by Railway Air Services, North-Eastern Airways, etc.

Handley Page "42." A veteran type used by Imperial Airways for many years and now being gradually replaced by modern machines. Still operates Le Touquet service and others.

Airliners regularly seen at Croydon Airport in 1939 include these as illustrated in a contemporary periodical.

Marcel Bloch "220" type, used by Air France. Top speed, 212 m.p.h.; 16 passengers; two engines of 890 h.p. each. Operate an hourly service to Paris.

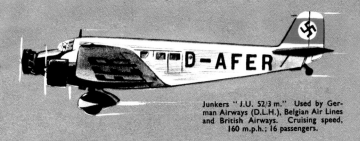

Junkers "J.U. 52/3 m." Used by German Airways (D.L.H.), Belgian Air Lines and British Airways. Cruising speed, 160 m.p.h.; 16 passengers.

Douglas "D.C. 3." American built air liner used by K.L.M., Swissair, Swedish Air Lines, etc. Top speed, 212 m.p.h.; 21 passengers.

Savoia-Marchetti "S.73." Italian type used by the Belgian Air Lines. Speed, 200 m.p.h.; 18 passengers; three engines, 600 h.p. each.

ALL ABOUT EUROPE'S FAMOUS AIR-LINES.

K.L.M. ROYAL DUTCH AIRLINES
BADGE

DOUGLAS D.C.3.

The Royal DUTCH Air Lines. Airports at Schiphol and Waalhaven. Luxury air-liners run daily services to all European capitals. Twice a week K.L.M. machines fly from Amsterdam to Batavia via Greece, Egypt and India. The famous Douglas D.C.3 air-liners are included in the K.L.M. air fleet of 51 planes. Civil marking on planes, PH—.

D.L.H. DEUTSCHE LUFTHANSA
BADGE

JUNKER J.U. 52.

Deutsche Luft Hansa is GERMANY'S number one air line. Network of regular air service throughout Europe. Main air-port Templehof. Co-operates with Graf Zeppelin in South Atlantic mail and passenger service. The up-to-date air fleet numbers 137 machines and includes the famous Junkers air-liners. Civil marking on planes, D—.

AIR FRANCE
BADGE

BLERIOT SANTOS DUMONT

Principal air line in FRANCE. Operates from Paris and Marseilles. Regular passenger and mail services to all European capitals. Bleriot Santos Dumont flying-boats cross the Atlantic to South America with mails. Weekly passenger services run to French Indo-China, and daily service to North Africa. Operates 93 machines. Civil marking on planes, F—.

AEROTRANSPORT
BADGE

DOUGLAS D.C.3

The SWEDISH Air Line operates with K.L.M., the main air-line between England and Scandinavia. The Douglas D.C.3 air-liners seat 21 passengers and do the London-Stockholm run in 7 hours. Regular service to Norway, Denmark and Berlin. Fleet of 9 planes. Civil marking on planes, SE—.

SABENA BELGIAN AIR LINES
BADGE

SAVOIA·MARCHETTI

BELGIUM'S national air line. Co-operates in the famous daily air-route from London across Europe to Rome. Uses Savoia-Marchetti machines in her fleet of 20 planes. Runs a weekly service from Brussels to the Belgian Congo, carrying mails, passengers and freight. Chief airport at Haren, Brussels. Civil marking on planes, OO—.

SWISSAIR
BADGE

DE HAVILLAND EXPRESS

SWITZERLAND'S premier air line fleet of ten planes. A daily service is run from Croydon to Zurich in collaboration with Imperial Airways. De Havilland Express and Douglas air-liners are used. Seven and fourteen-day air tours of the Alps are run, including flights over Mont Blanc and other famous peaks. Civil marking on planes, HB—.

Some of these pre-war names are still with us, such as Air France, Lufthansa and KLM, which is the oldest airline in the world still operating under its original name. Aerotransport joined the Scandinavian Airlines System in 1948, whilst SABENA became bankrupt in 2001 with Swissair, Switzerland's former national airline, ceasing operations in 2002.

Air mail plays an important part in Croydon's busy life. Special Post Office Air Mail vans of streamlined design transport the mail direct to the planes waiting on the tarmac. Over 40,000,000 letters are carried from Croydon annually.

The Air Ministry own the fire and ambulance appliances, one of each being stationed in readiness at the airport.

Tractors are used for turning the huge aircraft out of the hangars and on to the tarmac. They are of varying design, each company supplying its own type.

And if air enthusiasts ever became bored of spotting aircraft, they could always turn their attention to the ground transport facilities, as these period illustrations indicate.

Listening to the planes

Back at the beginning of radio broadcasting (the early 1920s) listeners had few stations to entertain them. Weekly programme papers included Croydon Airport in their listings of stations for tuning into. By the mid-1930s large numbers listened in on 862 metres for transmissions such as 'Passing Dungeness for Le Treport at 3,000 feet' and 'Hullo Imperial X Denmark, Croydon calling for your QTE. Switch on please. Over.' The 9 March 1935 issue of *Practical and Amateur Wireless* devoted half a page to explaining the cryptic codes and abbreviations, as well as how aircraft received their true bearings and weather forecasts.

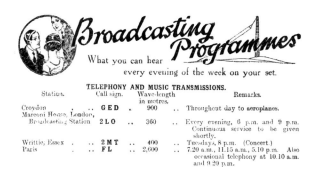

November 1922 was the month that the BBC began broadcasting. Anyone who bought *Popular Wireless Weekly* that month would have found Croydon Airport (callsign GED) heading the list of 'programmes'. How many people actually tuned in is a bit of a mystery but no doubt some did, simply out of curiosity.

The letter in these covers was carried around the world on the first joint Pan American and Imperial Airways air mail flight between 24 June and 28 July 1939. The route taken was New York–Shediac–Botwood–Foynes–Southampton–Cairo–Karachi–Singapore–Hong Kong–Manila–Guam–Wake Island–Midway Island–Honolulu–San Francisco–New York, using Boeing 314 Clipper and Short S23 flying boats.

Aerophilately

Specific air mail stamps and others depicting aeroplanes made an interesting theme for casual stamp collectors, whilst serious collectors could turn their attention to the special covers used to commemorate the opening of new air mail services. A number of these took a close interest in the development of air mail facilities, noting the date of new flights and destinations as they became available and posting specially prepared envelopes that would capture the special cancellations and stickers. In some cases the airline or postal authorities would produce special 'cachets' or designs for the occasion that might also be signed by the pilot of the inaugural flight. Obviously this entailed the sender knowing someone to receive — and return — his precious stamped letter but this might be a business connection. If not, a stamp dealer might undertake this task or as a last resort, the British Consul in the destination city might oblige.

These 'postal history' items are now highly collectable and traded on Internet auction sites, as are other postal novelties, such as the rather expensive three-shilling book of stamps issued by Royal Mail in March 1930, the first to include the little blue 'Air Mail Par Avion' labels that had to be stuck on envelopes containing air mail. People also collect air mail labels, air letter forms (aerogrammes) and the colourful advertising stamps that were widely added to envelopes in times gone by.

The Internet contains many websites devoted to aerophilately. Collectors who specialise in air mail material are served by the British Air Mail Society, whose lineage dates back to the Aero Philatelic Club, London (founded in 1923). Members receive a quarterly journal and take part in the society's own regular auctions.

Model Aircraft

Every picture tells a story so what did become of the young occupant? The 'director of Heston Aerodrome' was in fact Sir Nigel Norman, joint owner of Airwork Services and Heston Aerodrome and also jointly responsible for designing the buildings and lay-out of many municipal airports in the UK and overseas. In fact he had three sons, who all shared the endearing little aircraft shown above. G-WAWP clearly had a major influence on his sons, since Sir Nigel's first-born, Mark Norman rose to be company secretary of Bristol Siddeley Engines, whilst second son was Desmond Norman, co-founder of the aircraft manufacturer Britten Norman (seen in the picture above). The third son, philanthropist and vintage aeroplane collector Sir Torquil Norman earned his fortune from toy manufacturing.

He told the London *Evening Standard* in 2004: "My dad built Heston aerodrome, and my two brothers and I were brought up on the apron where Heston Service Station is now, on the M4. He built us a little biplane pedal car with G-WAWP painted on the side — God Willing and Weather Permitting — all very old-fashioned stuff."

Norman senior clearly had a well-developed and wry sense of humour.

Reading and playing

If the 1930s were the decade when adults become air-minded, then this was when boys became obsessed with aviation. Their comics featured plane-spotting guides and rip-roaring tales of plucky aviators, whilst articles in the *Meccano Magazine*, *Modern Wonder* and *Practical Mechanics* delivered informative technical data and background information. Christmas and birthday present books provided an opportunity for annuals and the Wonder Books to cash in on the same craze.

Aeroplanes — and model aeroplanes — held massive appeal for boys of all ages in the 1930s.

Toys of the period included small die-cast aircraft by Dinky Toys and other makers, balsawood aeroplanes to construct such as Lines Brothers' 'FROG' range, this acronym standing for Flies Right Off The Ground. These planes used rubber bands for propulsion, unlike the 'FROG Penguin' range, which were non-flying models for collecting. These were made of celluloid in 1:72 scale from 1936 onwards and have been claimed as the world's first plastic model construction kits. Enthusiasts could also construct aircraft out of Meccano parts but in 1931 the company introduced a series of purpose-made Aeroplane Constructor sets that included bespoke propellers, landing wheels and ribbed fuselage parts to make more realistic models. All of these toys are now sought after by collectors, particularly when they have been well cared for.

A great game for parties was Wings. Actually a card game, the challenge for players was to make the best use of cards they were dealt, handling mail and reacting to delays. Mail had to be delivered to cities in the correct sequence and the winner was the first player to get his or her mail to the final destination.

FROG Penguins, the world's first plastic model aeroplane kits, were sold as children's toys but were also ideal for identifying aircraft, as this 1939 advertisement indicates.

Next stop — New York! A giant Pan American flying boat, carrying passengers across the Atlantic, takes off from an aerodrome anchored in mid-ocean, on the second stage of its journey from the Old World to the New.

When this illustration was published in 1937 it was expected that construction of a refuelling and maintenance point would start in the next few months.

FLIGHTS OF FANCY

This chapter deals with unfulfilled dreams — the revolutionary schemes and projects that never quite made it. All of these 'might-have-beens' could have become reality were it not for the worsening state of international politics after 1936 and the war that broke out in 1939. Historically the first of these casualties was the notion that increased air travel could eliminate international tensions and eradicate future wars.

The First World War of 1914-18 was supposed to have been the war to end all wars and its bitter memories mean that many people never wished to see another conflict like it. In 1933 the annual conference of the Labour Party in Britain resolved unanimously to 'pledge itself to take no part in war'. The League of Nations (forerunner of the United Nations) preferred sanctions to aggression; its 'Peace Ballot' conducted in the winter of 1934-35 indicated that many millions of British people were overwhelmingly opposed to any return to conflict, with widespread support for pacifism.

A well-argued booklet published in 1934 made a powerful argument for establishing a World Airways corporation to take over national airline operations, with an international air ambulance service operated by the Red Cross. The abolition of bombing from aircraft would have been a welcome by-product.

However desirable this might have been, it was not to be. Italy's invasion of Abyssinia, the Spanish Civil War and Hitler's annexation of Austria put pacifism to a severe test. Despite the Munich Agreement of 1938, that led to the German occupation of the Sudetenland, and appeasement in Britain's foreign policy, the outbreak of war could not be avoided in September 1939.

WORLD AIRWAYS —WHY NOT ?

A PRACTICAL SCHEME FOR THE SAFEGUARDING OF PEACE

Report of a Committee set up by "Essential News" and the "Week-end Review" to examine the possibility of a World Air Transport Service and the abolition of Aerial Warfare

with a Foreword by
W. ARNOLD-FORSTER

LONDON:
VICTOR GOLLANCZ LTD
14 Henrietta Street Covent Garden
PRICE 1/- NET

World air services were a topic of debate in 1934. The Spanish Civil War of 1936-39 and events in central Europe soon put paid to peaceful aspirations.

New airports for London

One casualty of the outbreak of war was the standstill it brought to plans for the expansion of London's airport facilities. By the late 1930s it was clear that air travel was growing at a rate that would soon render none of the existing airports adequate. These airports were Croydon, from which Imperial Airways served the British Empire, and Heston, from which British Airways flights took off for European destinations. The facilities at Croydon had become somewhat dated and required updating. Room for expansion was limited and road congestion made travel inconvenient from central London. By 1939 Heston Aerodrome (on the Great West Road near Hounslow) had been developed to a size almost as large as Croydon but its site also offered insufficient capacity for expansion on the scale required. This led the government to create two additional brand new airports outside London in more rural areas. One of these was to be built at Lullingstone in Kent (between Swanley and Sevenoaks) and the other at Fairlop in Essex (north of Ilford). Both sites were located close to railway lines and each of the new airports was to have its own station, even though events turned out otherwise.

Construction of both of the new airports had been planned to start around the time when war broke out. It was decided that Fairlop should be built as an RAF fighter station, which became operational on 1 September 1941 (and closed in 1946, when it was considered the location was unsuitable for civil aviation). At Lullingstone the railway station was built ahead of the airport in expectation of housing development in the neighbourhood. It was virtually ready for opening and appeared in the summer 1939 timetable with no train times given but a footnote indicated that the date of opening would be announced. Work on the airport never began and the planned housing estate was held up by the war (and was never resumed on account of post-war Green Belt legislation). Over the decades the unopened and unused station crumbled away and most of the structure was removed in 1955, although the abandoned concrete approach road and the bulk of the platforms remain. Subsequent planning for London's airports is discussed in the next and final chapter.

Wings over the Atlantic
Aviation across the Atlantic was an early success, the first non-stop flight from the USA to the British Isles having been made already in 1919 by the British aviators Alcock and Brown, who were knighted for this achievement by King George V. With fuel and crew as the only payload, flights of this kind were perfectly feasible but not if the craft had to carry a full complement of passengers and mails.

Nevertheless transoceanic air travel from Europe to North America was considered a realistic possibility by the mid-1930s, with the proviso that aircraft would require to land for refuelling at mid-Atlantic 'seadrome' relay points. Also known as floating platforms and ocean airports, these constructions were first proposed in 1927 by the engineer and inventor Edward Robert Armstrong. The idea was discussed widely in both technical and popular publications, even becoming the subject of a science fiction drama film *F.P.1 Doesn't Answer* in 1933. In 1937 British publications were stating in all seriousness that construction of the first seadrome was no more than six months off.

Armstrong's seadrome was to take the form of a huge flying deck — nothing less than a floating aerodrome — supported on tubular legs that in turn rested on floats submerged deep in the water. The deck itself would stand high above the water and this, together with the fact that the buoys that supported the whole affair would lie too deep to be moved by weather conditions on the surface, would ensure than even when enormous waves were buffeting Atlantic liners, the aerodrome would remain as steady as a rock. Numerous variants of this design were devised, most of which included a hotel, restaurant, and technical facilities. One of these plans required just two seadromes in the Atlantic Ocean, one for each direction of flight, which would take account of prevailing winds and weather conditions. Outbound planes from Europe would land first at the Azores, on a seadrome and then in the Bermuda islands before reaching New York. The eastbound journey would touch down in Newfoundland, then on a seadrome and then in Ireland before reaching home.

The unexpectedly rapid development of longer-range aircraft that did not require intermediate refuelling points eliminated the need for midway seadromes of this kind. The dream of an Atlantic air mail and passenger service came true on 6 July 1937, when Imperial Airways' flying boat *Caledonia* reached Botwood (Newfoundland) 15 hours 3 minutes after leaving Foynes (Ireland). PanAm's flying boat *Clipper III* made the journey in the opposite direction even faster (in 12 hours 40 minutes), not having to fly into a head wind.

Armstrong's original thought was not wasted, however, since his concept of an anchored deep-sea platform was later applied to create floating oil rigs. Meanwhile Germany had deployed three service vessels termed seadromes by some (they were aircraft carriers and mother ships) on which Lufthansa flying boats of the South American mail service landed for refuelling and servicing. Named the *Westfalen*, *Schwabenland* and *Ostmark*, they were stationed in the 1930s off Brazil and the west African coast, and operated for Lufthansa by Norddeutscher Lloyd. Take-off was assisted by catapult.

Ice isles as airports

Another example of German innovation was the plan for a chain of seadromes in the Atlantic made of artificial ice. This was the proposal made in 1932 of Dr Arthur Gerke of Waldenburg, who decided that seadromes could be constructed at a fraction of the cost of previous schemes by using ice as a support platform. By creating a multi-layer cage of pipes in the sea cooled by refrigeration plant onboard ships, it would be possible to create a vast 'cake' of solid ice that could be maintained in its frozen state by compressors installed permanently on the platform constructed above. So he claimed, although nobody put his notion to test by constructing a seadrome of ice.

However, the idea was revived — with a crucial improvement — during the Second World War and this time it nearly came to fruition. The modification was the addition of sawdust to the formula (14 per cent sawdust, 86 per cent water), which transformed ice from a rather brittle material into 'pykrete', a composite material akin to concrete, with vastly improved strength and toughness. Its other remarkable property was the relatively long time that it took to melt, thanks to the low thermal conductivity of the sawdust component.

The original idea of English freelance inventor Geoffrey Pyke was to build aircraft carriers, constructed like floating islands, out of ice. He explained his concept with sufficient conviction that it had the approval of

Lord Louis Mountbatten, head of combined operations, and of his scientific adviser.

Churchill was also impressed, but had an even better idea according to historian Stephen Battersby: 'Why not just break off a flat piece of ice from the Arctic and tow that around as a mobile airbase?'

It was realised that pure ice would crack under the weight of aircraft but a solution came in a report by Herman Mark, an expert in physical chemistry who had escaped from the Nazis to the USA. This stated that that ice made from water mixed with wood fibres formed a solid mass that was much stronger than ice made of water alone. In 1943 a 1,000-ton prototype vessel was actually made in Canada with pykrete, as Pyke called the improved material but tests later proved that even this would have been inadequate to bear the weight of aircraft.

According to General Lord Ismay, the work had considerable merit. In his memoirs he recorded: 'A good deal of consideration, much of it highly technical, was also given to the feasibility of building floating platforms which could either be used by fighters to support opposed landings until such time as airfields ashore were available, or act as staging points for ferrying aircraft over long distances. ... The whole thing seemed completely fantastic, but the idea was not abandoned without a great deal of investigation. Various alternative methods of construction were then considered by the United States naval authorities, but in the end there was general agreement that carriers and auxiliary carriers would serve the same purpose more effectively.'

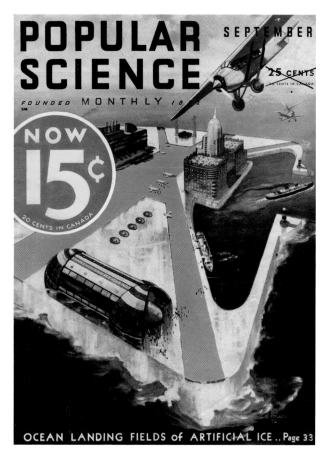

'Daring project would dot sea with islands kept solidly frozen' is how *Popular Science* magazine succinctly summarised Arthur Gerke's scheme to slash the cost of constructing mid-Atlantic seadromes in 1932. The notion was by no means fanciful; two years previously a sunken ship was raised from the bed of Lake Geneva, Switzerland, by forming a block of artificial ice within the hull. In 1943 a prototype ice construction was made in Canada.

EPILOGUE

The outbreak of war in September 1939 inevitably dealt a significant blow to air travel in and from the UK, although a number of services continued. For instance, scheduled flights by Isle of Man Air Services ceased temporarily at the outbreak of war, although the company was permitted to resume a limited schedule of flights from 20 November 1939 on the Isle of Man to Liverpool and Isle of Man to Belfast routes. However, the Belfast flights were soon suspended as a result of government orders prohibiting civil air traffic between the Isle of Man and Northern Ireland.

From 1 September 1939 a statutory department of the Air Ministry called National Air Communications managed civilian flying operations. Most civilian aircraft and support facilities were relocated away from London and other coastal districts. Services to Paris, Stockholm and certain other overseas destinations were allowed to continue. Airlines of neutral countries such as Belgium, Denmark and The Netherlands were permitted to use only coastal civilian airfields such as Shoreham Airport, whereas Air France continued to fly from Paris (Le Bourget) to London (Heston). There was even a new service in wartime, operated by Aer Lingus, between Dublin and Liverpool. This began on 19 January 1940, initially daily but twice weekly from 1941 until it was suspended in 1944.

Further intervention occurred on 5 May 1940, when the Associated Airways Joint Committee (AAJC) was set up to co-ordinate the air services of the seven UK internal airlines. Government and military passengers had priority over normal traffic. The airlines were confined to flying routes 'of national importance' (for example the Liverpool–Belfast–Glasgow route of Railway Air Services), carrying government and other 'priority' passengers and mail. Fare-paying passengers could travel on these flights only if government authorities were prepared to release the priority seats that they held.

New companies, new routes

British Airways Ltd and Imperial Airways were officially merged as a new company, British Overseas Airways Corporation (BOAC), on 1 April 1940 and on 4 June 1940 BOAC started a service from London (Heston) to Lisbon, connecting there with the transatlantic flying boats of Pan American World Airways.

The flying boat service operated by Imperial Airways from Southampton Docks was transferred to Poole on 1 September 1939 and continued to operate as required (from 1 April 1940 under the British Overseas Airways Corporation banner). A special train, known as the 'Imperial Airways Special' and made up of the luxurious Pullman coaches *Rosemary*, *Rosamund* and *Plato*, ran nightly from London to Poole to connect with a flying boat service to the USA. Maintained in immaculate condition, this train's passengers were diplomats, high-ranking service officers and civilian pilots returning to the USA after ferrying planes to England.

Following the Allied victory, the new Labour government in the UK announced plans on 1 November 1945 for a shake-up of air services in Britain. Civil flights were to be provided by three state-owned corporations: BOAC would continue to operate routes to the Empire, Far East and North America; British European Airways (BEA) would now operate services to Europe and domestically within the United Kingdom; whilst British South American Airways (BSAA, merged with BOAC in 1949) was to operate new services to South American and Caribbean destinations.

The Victory airport and Heath Row

With civil aviation poised to take on far greater significance, the plans of 1939 for four London airports were scrapped. The war years had provided plenty of time for contemplation, with thoughts turning to one or more 'terminal' airports, this being a buzz-word of the 1940s for facilities handling continental and intercontinental services. July 1943 saw speculative plans announced for a new £20 million Thames Estuary airport at Cliffe, a flat spot on the Kent Coast opposite Canvey Island. Avoiding the question of whether land planes or flying boats would predominate in the future, both land runways and an artificial lagoon were proposed, each providing a landing path two and a half miles long. It was estimated that the new airport would handle eight million passengers a year plus a large volume of freight.

Interest in the Cliffe proposal, by now styled the Victory airport and hailed as the largest and most modern airport in the world, peaked in May 1945. The *Daily Telegraph* dismissed the alternative plan concentrating Transatlantic flights at 'Heath Row', flying boats at Portsmouth and Continental services at Gatwick, commenting this 'would soon see the main [transatlantic] terminal established in Europe and Britain on a feeder line.' The uncanny similarity to current fears that Schiphol will dominate if the 'Boris Airport' is not constructed in the Thames Estuary hardly needs mentioning!

In the event Heathrow, then known as Heath Row (two words), was chosen as the main London Airport, and its proximity to Heston Aerodrome ruled out any resumption of flying from that location.

Thereafter Croydon and Gatwick airports played only a small role, Croydon closing in 1959 following a steady decline and Gatwick (used only for charter flights) in 1956

The description 'terminal' for an airport handing international flights crossed the Atlantic during the 1940s, being applied to the new London Terminal Airport proposal of 1945. In fiction Sherlock Holmes had already flown from London Terminal two years previously, in the futuristic Hollywood film *Sherlock Holmes in Washington*.

(it reopened two years later after massive rebuilding as a new airport for London). Heathrow became operational as the new London Airport in March 1946. The facilities were very much of the 'interim' variety, with passengers using army tents (marquees) and duckboards, replaced within six months by prefabricated buildings (the first permanent terminal was not opened until 1955). Construction continued in phases at Heathrow, while BEA and other European flagship carriers used the nearby Northolt air base until the central area at Heathrow opened in 1954.

Forward to 1950

Wartime restrictions on flying ended in January 1946 and peacetime civil flights resumed shortly afterwards, with some airlines (such as Railway Air Services) now employing newly acquired Avro Ansons and ex-RAF Douglas DC-3 Dakota machines, as well as a number of ex-German Luftwaffe Ju 52 tri-motor aircraft. The Civil Aviation Act of the same year created a nationally-owned carrier known as British European Airways, which was given the monopoly of scheduled air services within the United Kingdom and to continental Europe. It came into being on 1 August 1946. This signalled the beginning of the end for the existing private-sector airlines in the Associated Airways group. These companies operated their services on behalf of BEA until they ceased operations on 31 January 1947. The following day the state corporation acquired the aircraft, staff and routes of the four remaining airlines, which from then ceased to exist. BOAC was unaffected by these changes.

Aviation took on an entirely new significance in the post-war era and an entirely new era of flying began in 1946. On 1 February a BOAC Hythe flying boat made a 35,313-mile route survey from Poole to Australia, New Zealand, Hong Kong, Shanghai and Tokyo, whilst in the following month British South American Airways began a regular service from London to Buenos Aires via Lisbon, Bathurst, Natal, Rio de Janeiro and Montevideo using Avro Lancastrians. The first post-war UK to Australia flying boat service commenced in May, operated jointly by BOAC and QANTAS with Hythe flying boats, taking five and a quarter days. In July BOAC inaugurated its London-Shannon-Gander-New York route using Lockheed Constellations, the first British civilian flights on the North Atlantic. The first commercial BOAC operation to Canada commenced with a weekly Constellation service between London and Montreal, via Prestwick and Gander in April of the following year.

Aircraft had changed out of all recognition too. Airliners were larger, faster and more comfortable. New pressurised aircraft, such as the Canadair Argonaut, Handley Page Hermes and Boeing Stratocruiser, were able to fly above the weather, whilst passengers could fly from London to New York via Prestwick in under 20 hours. Many of the new machines were based on wartime transport aircraft and among the outstanding British commercial designs were the Bristol Brabazon (capable of 250 miles an hour, with capacity for 50 passengers and two tons of mail) which flew first in 1949 and the Avro Tudor II for transatlantic service and first flown in 1946. The latter, a landmark design, was noted at the time for its roominess, stylish passenger promenade and bar, together with a luxurious ladies' powder room. The furnishings and even the crockery all fulfilled the conditions laid down by the Design Council.

Finally, to mark the end of an era and of this book, in 1950 BOAC withdrew the airline's last flying boats. Following the tradition set by its predecessor Imperial Airways, it had maintained continuous flying boat operations since 1924.

 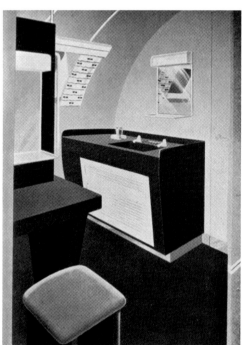

When the prototype Avro *Tudor II* made its maiden flight in 1946 (just one year after the end of hostilities) it was the UK's largest airliner and the first with a pressurised cabin. Dubbed a 'flying hotel' by the media, its internal accommodation was the last word in up-to-date design, good taste and luxury — as these photos of the bar area and ladies' powder room show.

Somewhat bleak is a fair description of the passenger reception facilities at London's Heathrow Airport in July 1946. Prominent are army tents for the check-in desks, a mobile post office and wooden duckboards for crossing muddy ground (the summer was particularly wet in that year). Fortunately prefabricated buildings had replaced this miserable encampment before the notoriously cold winter of 1946/7 set in.

INDEX